ILDA:

the chronicle of a Saint

HILDA:

the chronicle of a Saint

*A story of saints and kings,
and the beginnings
of the English church*

By
Anne Warin
Artwork by Sheila Mackie

Published by:
Marshall Pickering
Middlesex House
34-42 Cleveland Street
London W1P 5FB

Marshall Morgan and Scott
Lamp Press
34–42 Cleveland Street, London, W1P 5FB, U.K.

British Library CIP Data

Warin, Anne
  Hilda
  1. Christian church. Hilda, Saint, 614–680
  I. Title
  270.2′092′4

ISBN: 0–551–01908–5

Text Set in Linotron Ehrhardt by
Input Typesetting Ltd, London
Printed in Great Britain by
Cox and Wyman, Reading

CONTENTS

Oswy's accession and his marriage to Enfleda of
Kent. Hilda leaves Northumbria for East Anglia.
Aidan sends for her to return. She founds
Wearmouth, and later Hartlepool. The murder of
Oswin. Oswy's victory over Penda at the Battle of the
river Winwaed. The infant Elfleda is dedicated to the
church.

A SIMPLIFIED GENEALOGY OF THE NORTHUMBRIAN KINGS IN THE TIME OF HILDA

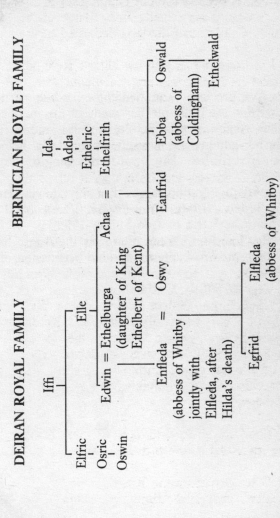

DEIRAN ROYAL FAMILY

Iffi

Elfric
Osric
Oswin

Elle

Edwin = Ethelburga
(daughter of King
Ethelbert of Kent)

Acha

Enfleda = Oswy
(abbess of Whitby
jointly with
Elfleda, after
Hilda's death)

Egfrid

Elfleda
(abbess of Whitby)

BERNICIAN ROYAL FAMILY

Ida
|
Adda
|
Ethelric
|
Ethelfrith

Eanfrid

Ebba
(abbess of
Coldingham)

Oswald

Ethelwald

Note

1. All that is known of Hilda's father, Hereric, is that he was a nephew of Edwin. Of her mother, Bregusyth, nothing is known except the story of her dream, as told by Bede.

2. Edwin had sons by an early marriage to a princess of Mercia, as well as the children born by Ethelburga. Oswy also had other children at the time of his marriage to Enfleda, notably Alcfrith, and Aldfrith who succeeded Egfrid. It is not certain if his daughter Alchfleda, married to Penda's son, Peada, was by Enfleda.

ACKNOWLEDGEMENTS

I have much appreciated the perceptive and constructive criticism that Pamela Gillespie has made of the manuscript in its various stages. Warm thanks are also due to Ruth Mitchell for her patient and painstaking secretarial help and to Dr Helen Byrt for her skilful word processing of the final draft.

I am grateful to Penguin Books Ltd for allowing me to quote from Bede's *History of the English Church and People* translated from the Latin by Leo Shirley-Price.

Dame Helen Gardner's translation from the Anglo-Saxon of *The Dream of the Rood* appears by kind permission of her literary executor.

A. W.

INTRODUCTION

My story is about Saint Hilda of Whitby. It is part fact and part imagination.

It takes place against the background of the conversion to Christianity, in the seventh century, of the Anglo-Saxons; those races who had infiltrated Britain, from across the North Sea, during the two centuries that followed the final departure of the Roman legions in the early fifth century.

It tells how the Roman traditions of Christian doctrine and liturgy, taught by the mission sent to the kingdom of Kent by Pope Gregory the Great under Augustine in AD 597, met, and were at last reconciled with the ancient traditions that already existed in the churches of Britain and Ireland.*

It tells how in the kingdoms of Northumbria especially, the Celtic monks from Iona and Lindisfarne played a major part in the conversion, and how a remarkable flowering of scholarship and art came about in the Northumbrian monasteries.

At no time in the history of the Church have women played so vital a role in its life as they did at the time of the Anglo-Saxon conversion and the years that followed. This was partly to do with the position of high-born women in Anglo-Saxon society. They were traditionally held to be the guardians of knowledge, who ensured the continuity of the cultural traditions of their race, and they were, by force of circumstance, able administrators of court and estate since their menfolk more often than not were slaughtered in battle. Their rights of property and inheritance were protected by law and they exercised considerable power in a society that was in many ways surprisingly sophisticated. They took readily to the new

*Appendix I describes the early British church as it existed at the time of the Anglo-Saxon invasions, and shows how the rather umbrella terms 'Roman' and 'Celtic' have come to be used.

faith and welcomed the access to learning that came with the missionary monks. The foundation of monasteries, and their administration in the role of abbess, was an ideal outlet for the wealth and inclinations of these women. Their ordination was of course never dreamed of, but they exercised considerable power in ecclesiastical affairs, and many of them became formidable scholars as a result of the great impetus to learning that was taking place through the exchange of scholarship with the continent and Ireland.

Such an Anglo-Saxon noblewoman was Saint Hilda, foundress of the monastery at Whitby in AD 657 and its first abbess. Born in AD 614, she was the great-niece of Edwin, king of Northumbria, one of the greatest of the Anglian rulers and the first to be converted to Christianity in the North. Her enigmatic figure stands at the very centre of events concerned with the conversion of our race, and no-one can measure to what extent she influenced its course.

Almost nothing is known of Hilda apart from Bede's account of her life and work in his *History of the English Church and People* written when memories of her were still fresh, and completed in AD 731, fifty-one years after her death.

She was baptised by St Paulinus at York, along with Edwin and his court, when she was thirteen years old. She was introduced to the Christian faith therefore through its Roman customs, because Paulinus had been sent from St Augustine's church at Canterbury with Edwin's Christian bride, the Kentish princess Ethelburga, to act as her chaplain and to undertake the conversion of the still pagan Edwin and his subjects as a condition of the marriage.

Bede does not tell us how Hilda spent the years after Edwin's death, only that 'Her life fell into two equal parts, for she spent thirty-three years most nobly in secular occupations, and dedicated the remainder of her life even more nobly to our Lord in the monastic life.'

How and where did she spend those first thirty-three years?

She would have been with her mother under Edwin's

protection after her father's murder, possibly in East Anglia during her infancy, where Edwin was in exile, certainly in Northumbria after his reinstatement there.

After Edwin's death in battle against the British in AD 632 she might have fled with Ethelburga and Paulinus to Kent, or to the protection of her sister Hereswith who had married into the East Anglian royal family. Yet something caused her to turn away completely from Roman to Celtic traditions of Christian doctrine and practice.

For this reason I feel certain that she must have remained in the North, coming under the influence of the saintly king Oswald who was reared, during exile, in the Columban traditions of Iona, while she carried out the administrative duties of a young noblewoman attached to his court. At the same time she would have encountered Aidan, appointed by Oswald to found the monastery of Lindisfarne, and his fellow missionary monks. Aidan knew and valued her enough to demand her return to Northumbria so that she could found a new monastery at Wearmouth, when she was already in East Anglia on her way to take vows at the monastery of Chelles in Gaul. The rule that she later introduced at Hartlepool, and then at Whitby, was in the Irish tradition of Iona and Lindisfarne. She represented the Celtic side at the Synod of Whitby, which she hosted in AD 664, although she was not called upon to speak. After it she became bitterly opposed to Wilfrid, that complex and fascinating personality, founder of the monasteries at Ripon and Hexham, who had so eloquently swayed the Synod in favour of Rome. As a leading authority in the Church Hilda was influential in the decision that led to Wilfrid's fall, in AD 678, from the temporal as well as ecclesiastical power that he had gained throughout Northumbria.

What sort of person was she, to return so obediently at Aidan's bidding when her mind was made up to follow a different course? Bede testifies to her 'wonderful devotion and grace', to her insistence upon the virtues of mercy, purity, peace and charity, and on an austere and simple way of life. He says that she was respected and consulted by leading ecclesiastics, and by kings and princes as well as ordinary folk: that there was high order of learning in her monastery and that its fame, with that of its abbess, spread far and wide.

She must have understood, and done everything to encourage, the link that lies between religion and art in all its forms; the function of art to reveal religious truth that is not expressible in the terms of everyday language. For she was so immediately perceptive of Caedmon's gift when she heard his verses that she at once called a high-level council to discuss how it might be used, and admitted the unlettered and ageing herdsman to the community as a brother, confident in his ability to learn the events of scripture and to turn them into song for the people. Archaeological excavation of the Saxon site at Whitby has revealed stone-work skilfully wrought with interlaced and animal decoration, traces of sumptuously bound and jewelled liturgical book covers and tools for illuminating manuscripts.

Using the primary evidence in Bede's writings, and in Edda's *Life of Wilfrid* and the findings of archaeology, and with the aid of modern histories, I have tried to be as accurate as is possible in a period that has left so few written records. Otherwise I have imagined personalities and events very freely.

For the sake of clarity familiar place names are used, such as Whitby, Ripon and York, although they derive from later times, and also the modern spelling of Anglo-Saxon names, since these come more easily to the tongue.

In some incidents the language of the translation from Bede's Latin (by Leo Shirley-Price in the Penguin edition of *A History of the English Church and the People*) has been too appropriate to change, and in the account of Edwin's vision at the court of East Anglia, of the arguments deployed at the Synod of Whitby, and in one or two other instances, I have quoted directly from the text.

Finally, where there are supernatural incidents in the story, I ask for a willing suspension of disbelief. Unless we can imagine in our own minds how these people thought, and therefore acted, we will not understand many of the events that took place.

It was an age of unquestioning faith. There was a readiness to find the will of God in natural events, and in smaller signs and coincidences that today would go unheeded. Columba believed that angels dwelt among the oak groves of his beloved Derry, and Bede that they were present at the services held in his church. Everyone knew that the departing souls of saints were carried to God by his angels, and it is not surprising that people saw this happen in their dreams. There was a total belief in the healing properties of holy relics, and force of suggestion explains certainly some of these miracles. Many of the supernatural events described by Bede in his history can be understood in these ways. The rest must remain in a dimension that is lost to us.

A Bibliography follows the Epilogue, and Appendix II is the Anglo-Saxon poem The Dream of the Rood, translated by Helen Gardner. There is disagreement among scholars as to Caedmon's authorship.

Anne Warin

PART I

The first thirty-three years

er Life fell into two equal parts, for she spent thirty-three years most nobly in secular occupations and dedicated the remainder of her life even more nobly to our Lord in the Monastic Life.

Bede, *A History of the English Church and People* IV 23:

CHAPTER 1

Like the cross-carpet pages, that precede each gospel in the Gospels Book of Lindisfarne, Britain at the beginning of the century that saw their making presented an intricate pattern of Christian and pagan culture. In the interweaving motifs of those pages, the threads of Christianity and of paganism are drawn together from origins that can be traced to the Mediterranean and Byzantium, to central Europe and to Ireland. Such also was the pattern in Britain itself, at the dawning of the seventh century.

The Christian faith had by no means reached throughout the land of Britain at this time. There were many still who clung fiercely to the old gods of their forefathers, particularly among the Anglo-Saxon races that for two centuries had infiltrated into Britain from across the North Sea. Nor had the native British people, who were by then largely Christian, attempted to evangelise the invaders. Paganism was a dominant motif still, within the pattern.

It was to pagan deities, and with pagan rites, therefore, that the noblewoman Bregusyth offered thanks for the safe delivery of her second child in the year AD 614. For she was of an Anglo-Saxon royal line, being wife to Hereric who was nephew to Edwin, deposed Anglian king of the southern Northumbrian province of Deira.

'Take the birth charms and return them to the priest,' she said to her serving woman Gode; round-faced Gode, born of a British slave-woman to a Saxon thane, who was of an age with her mistress and had served her since they were both children. 'Bid him prepare a libation for the earth-goddess, that he must pour into the River Wharfe where the

3

current runs swiftest, and into the fissure in the rocks where herdsmen saw a serpent vanish last summer, for so it will be taken deep into the earth where the great Mother dwells.'

She saw that the woman was reluctant to leave her, and added gently, 'You may leave me now for I am ready to sleep. The women have cared very well for me, and the child is strong and vigorous.'

Gode nodded, 'And I will send a messenger to tell Hereric also,' she said, wiping the sweat from her mistress's face with rough compassion, 'And the king, Cerdic, has asked to be informed.'

A shadow clouded Bregusyth's fair face. She did not trust the British king who ruled over Elmet; those lands that were bounded by the clear streams of Wharfe and Aire. At Cerdic's court Hereric and his followers had found uneasy refuge in their flight from Ethelfrith, king of the northern Northumbrian province of Bernicia, whose victory over his rival Edwin had forced the Deiran royal family into exile. Bregusyth knew that Cerdic's friendship for Edwin must be precarious, because Ethelfrith, fresh from a further victory over the British at Chester that had brought him close to Britain's western coast, was bent on further conquest. Cerdic, anxious for his own kingdom, was caught against his will in the struggle between the Anglian princes for the supremacy of all Northumbria; that territory that stretched from the marshy estuary of Humber to the deep inlet of Forth.

These princes claimed the ancestry of Woden. To their own people they were part king, part god. Ethelfrith was great-grandson of the pirate lord Ida, whose warriors for half a century had marauded inland from their foothold on the rock of Bamburgh. Edwin was the son of Elle, powerful lord of lands said to have been granted to him in return for aid to the Britons against other invaders, but much more likely seized from his allies in a coup. In a line and tradition of heroic warrior kings, they were fearless, proud, and bounteous to their own, but cruel and merciless to their foes even to the point of treachery to their own kin. It meant nothing

4

to either of them that Ethelfrith had taken Edwin's sister, Acha, as his wife. Bregusyth feared for her husband.

'It is well that the child is a girl,' Gode said quickly in comfort, lingering still when she saw that her mistress was troubled, 'she is far from the succession and Cerdic will take no thought to her birth.' For Edwin had heirs already in two sons born him by a Mercian princess in his youth, as well as in his nephew Hereric.

'It is well indeed,' replied Bregusyth, 'and moreover I think there is great need of women in these times, for the keeping of wisdom and learning lies in their hands. And I must not now endure the sorrow of a son slain or exiled as soon as he reaches manhood. But always I fear for Hereric. Send to him now, and he will inform Cerdic as he thinks fit, and later let Hereswith be brought to see her little sister.'

When Gode had gone she lay back upon the mantles and skins of her couch. Signs of the birth struggle had been cleared and fresh straw scattered in the small apartment. Curtains of fine woollen cloth separated it from the rest of the dwelling and others hung against the rough wooden walls, for Cerdic had housed them in a manner befitting their noble birth. It soothed her to hear the women talking together in low voices as they tended the cooking pot and the fire and watched over the child, washed and swaddled according to custom and sleeping now in a wicker-work cradle, and she drifted into sleep.

Quick footsteps, and a blast of cold air disturbed the curtains and blew in woodsmoke and the pungent smell of broiling meat and herbs. Hereric thrust into the apartment, filling it with his presence. Ruddy, panting, he tore off his heavy mud-splashed mantle and knelt awkwardly beside her.

'I was returning from the hunt,' he said 'when Gode hailed me. It is well with you? It is a fine child that lies sleeping there without, though I would have had a son, and we must soon get one in the making. But you are well, strong?' he asked again, and she felt an urgency, a tension in his bearing. She passed her hand reassuringly across his brow and smiled into his eyes, awaiting his next words.

'Bregusyth' he said in a low voice, 'I am no longer safe here. Ethelfrith will find some means of destroying any who stand between him and the kingdom of Deira so that all Northumbria may be his. Cerdic will not resist his bribes and his threats for much longer. If I should fly now then vengeance might fall upon you and the helpless children. So we must wait until you are strong enough for the long journey to join Edwin.'

Edwin and his forces had fled to East Anglia, hoping for an alliance with its powerful ruler, Redwald, against Ethelwald. Redwald at this time dominated the lands south of the Humber and claimed the title of Bretwalda, meaning High King, of the Anglo-Saxon tribes.

'If I could reach Edwin with my brave thanes and my own war skills we would score a noble victory.' Hereric's face flushed and his voice rose, 'And our babe shall be called Hilda, for it means Battle, and there will be mighty slaughter and Edwin lord at last of all Northumbria!'

Bregusyth placed a gentle finger on his lips. 'Husband,' she said, 'I wish that you would go alone, at once. Cerdic would not harm us. Without you we are no threat to Ethelfrith.'

But vehemently Hereric shook his head. 'Ethelfrith may offer him great rewards for my murder, land and precious goods, gold and silver finely wrought and gemstones that warm the heart. Cerdic might take revenge on you for their loss if I escape. I will not go without you.'

'Then I will match your courage,' she answered him proudly, 'and soon, a few days only, I will be ready for the journey. Gode shall begin to prepare in secret. Meanwhile let only Lilla wait on you. Trust no-one else. Go!' she said, 'for the evening feasting will soon begin, then come back to me to take your rest. And as for Hilda, why perhaps after this battle there will be peace.' But at this Hereric laughed aloud and kissed her and seizing up his cloak flung out through the curtain.

Ever watchful, Bregusyth grew strong and the babe fed hungrily at her breast, and the child Hereswith, watched over by the women, played with the other children among the thatched wooden dwellings of Cerdic's court.

But one day Hereric fell sick and did not return to her, sending a messenger to say that he had a grievous stomach disorder with great pain and would not disturb her rest but would stay with his thanes until he had recovered. Night fell, but she could not sleep and tossed restlessly on her pallet, neither could Gode soothe her, nor the sucking child comfort her. At last in the morning hours she fell into a fitful slumber and dreamed that it was summer and that she was walking with Hereric across the scented moorland, when suddenly he was no longer at her side. Terror such as she had never known clutched at her heart. Her garments seemed to impede her limbs so that she could scarcely move, but frantically stumbled searching among the barrows of those uplands, fearful that some ancient magic, or a god disturbed, had snatched him down into tombs where lay the bones of races who had peopled the land before the Romans came. Darkness fell, and exhausted at last she fell to the ground, and as she began to tear away the clothes that bound her limbs her fingers struck against something hard and ice-cold that lay against the warm flesh at her heart. Concealed beneath the folds of her garments was a mighty gemstone, lambent, glowing, greater than any she had seen among the jewels in the courts of kings. As she looked more closely it began to send forth beams of such brilliance that every corner of the landscape about her was bathed in a light that was brighter than the midday sun of summer, and the whole land of Britain lay like a map before her eyes lit up in its splendour. Her eyelids closed against the radiance and she fell into a deep untroubled sleep.

'My lady, you slept well at last,' said Gode, bringing the infant Hilda to her mistress at morning light.

'I have had a vision,' said Bregusyth. 'I think that Hereric is dead and that never again upon the earth will I feel his touch or hear his voice.' She bent her head upon the child folded in the mantle at her breast, 'But his child Hilda will be a great and shining light. Her life and works shall be an example to all who wish to live a good life throughout the land of Britain.'

'My lady,' said Gode, taking up the babe again and looking at the mother compassionately, 'Cerdic has sent for you to see him as soon as you can make yourself ready.'

Cerdic stood broad, close-knit, swarthy, akin to the races who lived in the wild country of the far west, but with the blood of the Roman conquerors mingling too in his veins. He saluted Bregusyth with the respect due to her rank but he would not meet her eyes.

'Hereric is dead,' he said abruptly. 'Last night. You know that he was sick. It was fetid meat perhaps, or roots or berries that some slave knew not were poison and threw in ignorance into the pot.'

Grief bowed her, but quickly she threw back her head. 'And were others sick from the same pot?' she cried, fierce-eyed.

'I know not,' he said, shifting uneasily from her gaze. 'But now it is over and you must return to your kin, to Edwin in East Anglia. The journey will take many weeks for you must travel by land, the storms now are too great at sea and I would have you go at once. The roads of my ancestors will serve you for much of the journey. Hereric's own thanes shall guard you and you will be well guided and provisioned. I will send messengers ahead to warn Edwin of your coming.'

'It is well for you own sake that you make such provision,' she answered proudly. 'I would not care to be one to suffer Edwin's vengeance, should any harm befall us.'

Cerdic flinched and with a sudden gesture took from his breast the charm that lay against it. It was a boar's tooth mounted in finely chased silver, that hung round his neck from a chain of silver links.

'Take it,' he said, 'and wear it on the journey. The smiths shall fashion me another. And now go.'

Bregusyth had no wish for his favours but she knew the protective power of such a charm and thinking of her children and of the journey before them she took it quickly from his hand and turned away so that he should not see she wept, and went out.

Standing outside was the thane Lilla: red-headed Lilla, ready to die for the sons of Woden. Tears sprang to his eyes when he saw her own.

'My lady,' he said, 'I guarded him closely, my body at all times ready to come between his and the sword thrust. I did not think to taste his food, for it was a common pot. Someone must have slipped an evil potion upon his meat unseen, as soon as it was served. Ah, that he should die so, and not as a hero in battle, and would that I had died in his stead! But Edwin will take revenge and I will be at his side. Now my life is at your service until you are safe with him. Already I have wagons preparing and Cerdic is providing well for us, for he fears Edwin. Bid Gode begin her preparations, and do not stint yourself for serving women and all that is needful for yourself and the babes. Cerdic must provide wagons and pack animals enough. We will leave immediately the burial rites have been performed.'

At first the travellers followed the track that skirted the upland region of Cerdic's kingdom, taking advantage of its valleys for shelter and of its forests and streams for fish, deer and goat, for meat. At night great fires were lit for protection against wild animals and often the company was merry for there were those among them who could sing, and others who had memorised the long alliterative lines in which the ancient tales were told. Then Bregusyth's spirits would revive a little, for she loved the music, and the matter of the poems, but still she grieved for Hereric and especially that because he had stayed at her side he had met so ignoble a death.

Then they struck east into a less sheltered country where

9

the cold winds blew from the North Sea across the marsh-lands of the Humber and the plain beyond. But Lilla and the servant Gode had planned carefully, loading the wagons with poles and skins to make shelters, and wood for fire, and Bregusyth and the little ones travelled snugly in a wagon covered with leather to keep out the cold.

The road left by the Romans, that had once joined their cities of Doncaster and Lincoln, was badly decayed, but it was raised, dry and straight, with causeways across the rivers Calder, Don and Idle, flowing on their courses to the Ouse and the sea.

So they came to Lincoln and found the city still part inhabited by those who had used its ruins as shelter for their homesteads, but in other parts the fallen columns and toppled stones of once mighty buildings mouldered in silent deso-lation so that some of the party drew back in terror and would not enter, thinking it to have been a habitation of giants. But Lilla, who knew the ruined Roman fortress of York, in Deira, laughed at them and told how the Romans had built their cities of stone, but how the art of dressing and cementing it was now lost; and so they entered and found good shelter there.

Bregusyth was wrapt in wonder at the fallen might and for a long time she stood musing before a finely carved pediment that was still supported on its columns. She was trying to understand the story that the weathered figures told of men and gods of another tradition and culture when movement in the darkness behind the columns startled her, and Gode at her side cried out in fear, and Lilla, ready to die for her and never far away, ran to thrust himself before her.

Out of the shadows there emerged two men, ill-clad and lean, but with something in their faces and bearing that arrested Bregusyth's attention so that she bade Lilla put away the sword that he had drawn. The men approached, holding out both hands to show that they were weaponless. They carried nothing but a small wallet each, of leather. Round their necks wooden crosses hung from thongs of plaited grass, and their heads were tonsured in a manner that left

10

the front part shaven back to a line from ear to ear. One was old and very frail, and his companion, many years younger, bore across his cheek and chin a livid scar that disfigured the lower part of his face, but his gentle eye and voice belied his sinister appearance as soon as he spoke.

'We beg a little food,' he said in the Anglo-Saxon tongue, but haltingly, 'We have travelled far and my companion, Bradan, is near fainting.'

'Certainly you shall eat with us,' said Bregusyth, 'and have rest and shelter too.' She turned to Lilla but he held up a hand in warning.

'They shall eat,' he said, 'but before they linger here I must know who they are and where they have come from.'

'We are Christian monks,' said the younger man, 'we come from the far west, from the monastery at Bangor where many hundreds of us follow a rule of prayer and study, and toil for our subsistence. We were among those few who escaped Ethelfrith's slaughter when he raised his army at Chester to defeat the Britons in those parts. I myself received a near-mortal wound, whose scar you see. The monks had assembled in a place apart to pray for the deliverance of the Britons from the heathen enemy, but Ethelfrith, fearing a power that he did not understand, directed his first attack against us, and those who had been put to guard us fled. My name is Botulf and I was born in these parts, and my companion is Bradan. He came to us in Bangor from Ireland where there is great learning among the monks. He is a scholar of Latin, and even of the Greek language, so that he can interpret and expound the Gospels of Jesus Christ by which we live, and the teaching and liturgy laid down by the early fathers of the church, but he does not understand your language as I have learned to do. Now we wander as pilgrims for Christ, seeking food and shelter only sufficient that our bodily needs do not distract us from our life of prayer and study. Soon God will call Bradan to return to Him and I will seek again the monastic life.'

Christian monks had reached the shores of Britain long before this time, confirming the rumours first brought, no-one knows how soon in those first centuries after Christ, by unnamed Roman soldiers. Very early there was an established church, that before long had known martyr, saint and heretic. Then into the far north west there came followers of those anchorites who once sought refuge in Mediterranean deserts from the persecuted church in Rome in its earliest days, and from the conflicts of doctrine that had beset it from the first. Braving uncharted seas and hostile coasts they searched out remote retreats where sometimes alone and sometimes in small communities they followed their calling to asceticism and learning. Here they developed a sturdy independence of organisation and practise, while always remaining faithful to the essentials of doctrine and liturgy laid down by the first councils of the Church. Such were the two monks, Botulf and Bradan. Then there were others, missionaries from Italy and Gaul, who brought to southern and eastern parts of the island a faith more closely allied in its organisation to the church in Rome. Within the growing design of Christianity itself, therefore, as it absorbed into its pattern the symbols and some of the rites of paganism, were branches that had spread out in many directions from the Tree of its Founder.

'I have seen something of this Christianity,' Lilla replied to Botulf, 'For I was in exile with Edwin for a time at the court of Ethelbert in Kent. I know that Ethelbert was converted to your faith by Augustine who came to these shores from Rome, sent by Pope Gregory. Edwin will have none of it, for he fears the vengeance of our gods should we abandon them, but Redwald, lord of East Anglia, was greatly stirred by Augustine and contrives to worship both your God and his own.' He laughed, 'It is said that he has set up altars bearing the symbols of Christianity on one face and those of our own gods upon the other. Especially among the Britons there are those who have forsaken their ancient gods for this god of yours. But it is said that the customs of the British Christians are not those that Augustine would see followed, and that the slaughter at Chester was the wrath of your own god falling upon you because your bishops will not accept the rulings of Rome.'

'Be that as it may,' said Botulf, 'I think that the differences that have grown are of no great importance. We follow closely and faithfully the rules and liturgy of the first councils of the Church, and in the study of the Gospels there are no barriers.'

'Eat with us now,' said Bregusyth, 'for you are hungry, and Bradan must have rest, and then there is so much that I would learn from you.'

So it was that Bregusyth learned of the Christian faith, and held in her hand the precious Gospel book that the two men had saved from Bangor. She was filled with longing to understand the fine formal characters of the script, copied in a thick dark ink onto parchment by the monks of the scriptorium at Bangor, and bound in black leather. She found herself telling Botulf all that was locked in her heart and especially of the dream that she had, concerning the infant Hilda. She led him to the dwelling that Gode and the women had contrived for her, and where they tended the little girl Hereswith and the baby Hilda, who was fast growing into a stout infant. Hereswith, fearful of the monk's distorted face ran to hide behind Gode, but the baby smiled a radiant toothless smile and clutched the finger that the monk held out to her. His own face lit up, so that Hereswith was persuaded to come from her hiding and look at him more closely, and he placed a hand upon each little head.

'Hold fast to your dream,' he said tenderly, turning to Bregusyth. 'You go to a heathen court and it may be that the understanding that you long for will be denied you and that your hope must be in these children. See that they receive instruction from any who may come to the courts where you will live, and guard them well for God has need of them. May it please him that our paths will cross again one day.'

So they parted with the monks and set out again, turning south along the raised causeway that took them next to Peterborough and so avoided the treacherous swamplands that lay inland from the Wash and were said to be the haunt of dragons. And in the woodland the early summer flowers began to bloom, and softer winds caressed the travellers, and the sun gleamed on patches of water left by the rains of spring. Bregusyth felt new strength and less pain when she remembered Hereric, and his youth and comeliness and how despite his pride and strength he would turn to her for help, for she knew that princes of the royal race must die in the flower of their youth. And she remembered what Botulf had said, and rejoiced and hoped for her children.

From Peterborough they turned east again, keeping to the way left by the Romans across the fens and so coming to Thetford where settlements along the south bank of the river Ouse carried a thriving trade with the continent, in precious stones and metals and in pottery, wool, cloth and honey. Here messengers from Edwin met them on the way, bearing provisions to ease the last part of the journey, and they knew that it neared its end. That evening there was feasting and song, and when the mead was flowing Gode was persuaded to dance; round-faced Gode moving with heavy feet to the rhythm that pulsed within her, that bound her to the growing crops and the warm earth and the bones of those long buried beneath it.

And so at last they came to the palace of Redwald, built upon the banks where the river Deben flows through dune and marshland to the sea.

14

CHAPTER 2

Edwin, deposed lord of Deira, prepared to receive the travellers with the ceremony that was dear to his heart. In the great hall, that stood at the centre of Redwald's stockaded royal township, he awaited them.

The timbers within the hall were hung with furs and woven wall-hangings, and silken hangings partitioned the apartment at its furthest end. Before these Edwin stood, a young man still, handsome and proud of bearing. His mantle, dyed a deep crimson from the dye made from cockles, was fastened on the shoulder by a disc brooch decorated with bands of golden filigree that enclosed precious stones and coloured enamel in an intricate geometric pattern. Gems glowed in the belt buckle that clasped a tunic trimmed with bands of gold-embroidered silk, and in the matching buckles that fastened his soft leather shoes. Beside him a thane stood guard over his war-gear; the gilt-crested iron helmet inlaid with silver wire, the two-edged sword in a leather scabbard overlaid in gilt-bronze with its hilt decorated by a pattern of interweaving snakes and vine leaves, the metal ornamented wooden shield, the chain-mail corslet, the spear and battleaxe.

At his other side stood the high priest Coifi, ready to perform the rituals of thanksgiving for the traveller's arrival in the temple that stood beyond the hall.

Overjoyed to see his lord again and to have delivered his charge without mishap, Lilla led in Bregusyth and threw himself at Edwin's feet and bowed his red head to the ground.

'My lord,' he cried, 'I am returned and my life is again at your service and for you I will die. I have brought brave

15

thanes with me and we are ready to return to take vengeance on Cerdic and to pursue Ethelfrith. At once, tomorrow, if that is your wish!'

But Edwin raised his hand in caution. 'We must remain patient,' he replied in a low voice, 'Redwald seems a generous and loyal ally but he will not yet commit himself wholly to our cause. Messengers have come in secret more than once from Ethelfrith, offering great rewards for my betrayal for he knows the way to Redwald's heart and Redwald is much tempted to add to his great treasury. Without firm promise of his army I cannot risk encounter with Ethelfrith, for the next battle must not fail. But you shall stay now at my side Lilla, and be first in my councils. This I promise.'

He turned to Bregusyth and took her hands in his. 'Lady,' he said, 'Redwald's queen has made fitting provision for you in the women's quarters, and you and your little ones will always be under my protection and your rights and inheritance guarded by our laws. One day we will find your daughters good husbands, noble princes perhaps among the sons and nephews of Redwald. As for yourself, you are still young and beautiful, and I will find you another valiant lord.'

At this Bregusyth paled, but held her head bravely and looked him in the eye.

'My lord Edwin,' she said, 'I would not have it so, and I ask your favour to let me remain unseen in the palace. In the women's quarters I can find much to occupy me.'

Edwin shrugged, 'Be it as you wish,' he said, 'you shall not be troubled by suitors if you do not desire it. Care well for your children and see that they learn the skills that they will one day need in administering royal lands and households, and in the dispensing of wisdom and justice among the people and in preserving knowledge, for such is the task of nobly born women and in these matters we depend upon them heavily.'

So Bregusyth took her place among the women of Redwald's court and was seldom seen in the township, for a great weariness had overcome her once the long and arduous journey was over and she knew that her children were safe.

16

She busied herself with overseeing the women at their tasks, but as time passed she fell to daydreaming and loved most of all to gather the children of the palace about her and to tell them stories; and she was spared her obligation to attend the queen in handing the drinking horn and the gifts at the feasts, in case any one should see her and ask Edwin for her hand against her will.

It was during the following winter, when the savage east wind blew from the sea and fierce waves lashed the sand-dunes, that a messenger came to Bregusyth from Edwin saying that a stranger was at the gate and asking for her with great insistence. The man would take no refusal from the guards, who would have driven him off for his uncouth appearance. But he had confounded them with a quiet authority so that, at a loss what to do, they had sent word to the king, and Edwin, close guarded by this thanes, went down to the gate himself.

Lilla, waiting to die for Edwin, was disappointed to recognise the young Christian monk Botulf, of the scarred face, who they had encountered in Lincoln during their journey, for he knew that he was a man of peace. Edwin, always watchful for an assassin in disguise, was still suspicious, but there was something about the man that filled him with that unwilling trust that he remembered from his encounter with the Christian monks in Kent. Besides, he would do much to please Bregusyth for she was becoming frail, no-one knew why, and was much loved for her wisdom and justice even to the lowliest of the slaves so that there was already greater trust between Redwald's household and his own.

'She shall be sent for,' Edwin said to the monk, 'and you may stay and rest here, but for one night only. Tomorrow you must go, however cruel the gale, but,' and he glanced at the monk's threadbare garment, 'you shall take away whatever provision Bregusyth sees fit to give you.' He waited only to see Bregusyth's joyful recognition of Botulf when she was brought and then, leaving them closely guarded, left him in her care.

Bregusyth was deeply concerned for Botulf for he seemed

half-starved so that the bones showed through his skin and his scarred face was haggard, but he would accept no more than the simplest of refreshment and some bread to carry with him the next day, and a goat's fleece to throw about his shoulders. He told her that his companion, the old scholar Bradan, had died in Lincoln in the first cold of the winter and that he himself was now on his way to the monastery of Chelles, near Paris, for he knew of it as a seat of learning where he could continue the studies into which Bradan had initiated him. Walking both day and night, with little food or shelter from the winter weather, he had reached Thetford where the traders had promised him passage in one of their vessels as soon as the wind should drop a little, and it was while awaiting this that he had thought of seeking her out in Redwald's palace.

'I have thought very much about the things you told me of, concerning your faith,' Bregusyth said to him as soon as he was refreshed, 'and I have tried to learn more from those of Redwald's court who were with him in Kent when he received Christian baptism. But you will know that when he returned here the queen and other advisers persuaded him to apostasise from the faith, fearing the revenge of our gods, for in disclaiming them he must also disclaim his own sacred ancestry. Yet still there stands a Christian altar in the temple outside the hall, beside the one that serves for sacrifices to our gods. And at the great feasts Redwald loves to use precious vessels bearing Christian signs, silver bowls chased with the cross and silver spoons that the treasurer has explained to me are engraved with the names Saul and Paul in Greek letters, which is the sign of conversion. But I dare not betray my interest in these matters to the queen for she shows great care and concern for us, and I think that my children must be brought up knowing only of the ancient gods of our race.

'But now, in the short time that remains before you rest ready for tomorrow, there are many things in my mind that I would question you about, and I long to touch again the holy book that you carry with you.'

18

So Botulf took the book from the leather wallet that hung from the girdle of his habit and read to her passages from the Gospel of St Luke, translating haltingly from the Latin into the tongue of the Anglo-Saxons as he went along, and pausing often to answer the questions that sprang to her lips.

'Perhaps when my children are grown I may bring them to Chelles,' Bergusyth said wistfully when the time came for him to leave her, 'for you say that nuns there, as well as the monks, study the scriptures.'

But Botulf looked at her in sorrow for he was struck by the great change that he saw in her.

'I think we may not meet again,' he said gently, 'but remember my words, that your hope must be in your children, and if it is denied to you to come yourself then one day perhaps God may call them to follow a life of holiness there.' And bestowing a blessing on her and on the little girls, he went on his way.

Two years passed and Hereswith and Hilda grew and thrived and the cheerful Gode watched over them. She taught them to sing and to dance and told them the stories of the gods, and they found playmates among the children of Redwald's household. And Redwald's queen who saw how frail their mother grew, cared for them too, and observing Hilda's keen intelligence even at so early an age, and the strong will that sometimes led her into trouble with her companions, would often take the child with her as she went about her duties.

Still Edwin bided his time, and Redwald, High King of the East Angles, waited and watched to see how he might further increase his kingdom and his wealth, for always he was torn between the demands of his honour and pride and those of his ambition and greed. Sometimes envoys came to him from Ethelfrith in secret, offering greater bribes and threatening war if his demands were refused, until at last Redwald, either corrupted by the one or intimidated by the other, agreed to betray Edwin. But Lilla had never ceased his vigilance, and discovering the plot he came to Edwin by night as his lord was about to lie down for sleep, and calling

19

him from his room warned him of the king's treachery, and implored him to escape from the province immediately with himself as guide to a place of safety from both Redwald and Ethelfrith.

Edwin thanked him, 'But I cannot act as you suggest,' he said. 'I cannot break the agreement I have made with so great a king, who has so far done me no harm, nor showed any hostility towards me. If I must die, I would rather die by his hand than by a hand less noble. For what refuge remains for me, who has already wandered for so many years in every corner of Britain trying to escape the hatred of my enemies?'

Lilla saw that he would not persuade the king and sorrowfully left him to take his rest, but Edwin remained alone outside the palace, brooding over his lost hopes, not knowing where to turn.

Redwald's queen lay at her husband's side greatly troubled, for she knew the forces that struggled within him and she understood that he had come to some decision that he feared to tell her. Gently she talked to him, of his sacred kingship and his majesty, of his honour and his justice, until he could no longer refrain from telling her of what he had done.

'My lord,' she cried, 'how can so great a king sell his best friend for gold, and worse still sacrifice his royal honour, the most valuable of all possessions, for love of money?'

Redwald could find no words to answer her and uneasily they turned away from one another, but at morning light the queen awoke to find him gone, and she knew that he had forsworn the unworthy plot and would at last give Edwin his full support.

Allowing the envoys to go, unsuspecting of his change of heart, Redwald was already preparing his army so that Ethelfrith could be taken by surprise. Proudly the queen went about her own rituals, proudly she helped to arm her young sons, and did not restrain them from riding to a battle from which she knew well they might not return.

With joy Lilla returned with the tidings to Edwin and found him still sitting alone in the place where he had left

20

him, but with his dejection changed to an expression of hope and amazement.

'Since you left me so downcast,' he said, 'I have had a vision that greatly heartened me and now this news that you bring throws some light upon its meaning.'

He told Lilla that at dead of night he had been much alarmed by the approach of a being whose face and garments were strange to him and who greeted him and asked the cause of his lonely brooding at such a time and place. When Edwin asked what concern this might be of his, the man replied, 'Do not think that I am unaware why you are sad and sleepless and why you are keeping watch alone. I know very well who you are, what your troubles are, and what coming evils you dread. But tell me this: what reward will you give the man who can deliver you from your troubles and persuade Redwald not to harm you or betray you to death at the hands of your enemies?'

Edwin answered that he would give any reward in his power in return for such an outstanding service.

Then the other went on: 'And what if he also promised you that you should become king, defeat your enemies, and enjoy greater power than any of your predecessors who have ever ruled in Britain?'

Heartened by these enquiries Edwin readily promised that, in return for such blessings, he would give ample proofs of his gratitude.

The stranger then asked a third question: 'If the man who can truthfully foretell such good fortune can also give you better and wiser guidance for your life and salvation than anything known to your parents and kinsfolk, will you promise to obey and follow his salutary advice?'

Edwin at once promised that he would faithfully follow the guidance of anyone who could save him out of so many troubles and raise him to a throne. On this assurance the man who addressed him laid his right hand on Edwin's head, saying: 'When you receive this sign, remember this occasion and our conversation, and do not delay the fulfilment of your promise.'

21

Hereupon he vanished, and Edwin realised that it was not a man, but a spirit who had appeared to him.

So at last the time for action had come, and in the autumn of the year AD 616 Edwin and Redwald led their forces against Ethelfrith. Surprising him before he could muster all his men at the southern border of Deira close to the Roman bridge across the river Idle, they defeated and killed him. His nobles fled, taking his young sons Eanfred, Oswald and Oswy, and his daughter Ebba, into exile in the northern provinces of the Scots and Picts, so that Edwin not only reclaimed his own kingdom but also gained the province of Bernicia, thus uniting all Northumbria. Redwald returned in triumph to his own kingdom, bearing home to the queen the body of one of her sons who had died a hero's death at his father's side.

Then a new life began for Hilda and her sister, for as soon as the spring weather came, and the necessary preparations could be made, Edwin's household left the palace of Redwald in a great baggage train of pack-animals and wagons, and set out on the long journey north to join the king.

Bregusyth did not accompany them. Her failing strength was not equal to such travelling and she knew now that soon she would die. Gently she had detached herself from her children, and Hilda, scarcely three years old, would not have remembered her mother for long had not the faithful Gode kept her memory always fresh in the child's mind.

Bregusyth knew that those who had care of her children understood well what was expected of royal princesses, and that Edwin himself would oversee their upbringing, and she treasured the memory of the dream that had come to her in Hilda's infancy, and died in the tranquil hope of its fulfilment.

22

CHAPTER 3

After his long years in exile, Edwin was now among the greatest of the kings in Britain, equalled in power only by his ally Redwald, and treated with respect by the princes of the midland kingdom of Mercia and by the heirs of Ethelbert, who had died in his kingdom of Kent in the year preceding Edwin's victory. Brave and ruthless, Edwin did not forget the injustices that he had suffered, and his loyal retainers gloried in bloody expeditions against those who had threatened his life. Urged on by Lilla he soon took vengeance upon the British king Cerdic for the murder of Hereric, driving him into exile and annexing the kingdom of Elmet.

Dearly Edwin loved pomp and ceremony and understood its value in inspiring awe among his people. Ancient tales of the panoply of Rome had reached his ears and it was in the manner of a Roman Emperor that he rode throughout his realm in the company of his thanes, his royal standard borne before him. And if he wished to pass through the streets of his townships on foot then the personal standard that the Romans had called a 'Tufa', a winged globe fashioned from precious metals and mounted on a spear, was carried in front of him as the symbol of a High King. With acts of kindness too he bound the people to him. Concerned for the refreshment of travellers, he ordered the erection of posts with brass bowls hanging from them in places where clear springs of water were adjacent to the highway, and no one dared use them for any thing except their proper purpose. And it was said that a woman could carry her newborn babe across the island from sea to sea in safety, so heavily would Edwin's justice fall upon any who molested her.

23

In the northern part of his realm Edwin's capital was the fortified township of Yeavering which lay sheltered in the foothills of the Cheviots. In the southern province he made his capital in the region of York, where some of his people had settled and made use of the still standing buildings of the Roman fortress. The east coast was guarded by the stronghold of Bamburgh, and Edwin's household moved with him between these royal palaces.

Hilda grew strong and independent and Edwin quickly recognised her keen intelligence. He watched over the children closely when he could, for he was frequently away from his court. He would explain to them, so far as their childish understanding would allow, about the sacred origins of their dynasty and the laws and traditions of their race, and as Hilda grew older she showed a passion to learn more, asking questions that he could not always answer so that he would become impatient and bid her put her mind to more important matters and to keep such questions for the women. As soon as they were old enough he allowed the sisters to stand beside him with the noble ladies of his household, richly clothed and wearing the royal gold and gemstones, to welcome the guests to his feasts with the cup and with gifts. But Hilda had no care for such adornment and bore it awkwardly, though she admired its beauty and craftmanship. Hereswith showed a greater grace on such occasions and Edwin saw in her a means of strengthening his alliance with Redwald, and began negotiating her marriage with one of the East Anglian royal princes as soon as she should be old enough.

Hilda began to understand how the court and the royal townships were administered. She watched the processes of cloth-making; the spinning and the weaving, and the skills of those who embroidered fine wool and silk. She saw how the women slaves, who were mostly of British origin, ground the meal and made dough for bread, how they brewed ale and made cheeses and butter for the king's table, keeping the buttermilk for themselves and for the herdsmen. She saw how frugal was their own allowance of food and ale and clothing, and how ruthless the laws that regulated it. She saw that there was a great difference between her own life and that of the poor, and she burned with pity for them although she was only a child. She loved them for the happiness that they found, despite their hardships, in making music, in dancing and in story-telling, for sometimes Gode would take her to watch their revels. Strong-willed and imperious she demanded that scraps from the royal table be taken to those in greatest need, and that the healing remedies made from herbs and roots were given to the sick. And Edwin, seeing how such care drew the people to him, ordered that her whims should be indulged.

Sometimes merchants would come to the court and the king's stewards would bargain with them, purchasing precious goods of rare design from countries that lay far beyond the coasts of Britain. Sometimes Christian monks would seek food and shelter, and because they were always poor and hungry and because Gode had told her about the monk Botulf, whose learning and talk had so deeply stirred her mother Bregusyth, Hilda insisted that they were well cared for. But the high priest Coifi saw to it that she did not talk to them, and sent them on their way as soon as they were refreshed.

Then, in the year AD 625, when she was eleven years old, another great change occurred in Hilda's life. In that year Redwald died and Edwin became the most powerful of the English kings, his influence extending into all the lands south of the Humber, excepting only the kingdom of Kent. Driving the native Britons from their territories he had pushed as far west as the islands of Anglesey and Mann, though he could not finally subdue the British ruler Cadwallon, who had retreated to the mountain fastnesses of Gwynedd, nor for a moment must he be unwary of the constant threat from Penda, rival Anglian lord of the midland kingdom of Mercia, as ambitious as Edwin himself but not as yet so powerful.

Hereswith's betrothal to one of Redwald's heirs had secured Edwin a footing in the East Anglian court, and next he began to look towards the court of Kent, where Eadbald the king was proving a less effective ruler than his father

Ethelbert, to see how he might make a claim to its power in the south and share in its links with the continent. To this end he sent an embassy of nobles to request from Eadbald the hand of his sister Ethelburga in marriage, and as soon as they returned to the royal palace at York with Eadbald's answer Edwin sent for Hilda.

At eleven years old Hilda had a gift of understanding and an ability in administration beyond her years, and was held in respect and affection by the people. Edwin was beginning to depend upon her and to allow her to attend at certain of his councils, for in some matters she already showed a greater wisdom than others among the noble women of the court. Bravely she had endured the parting with her sister Hereswith, sent now to learn the ways of the East Anglian court under Redwald's formidable queen so that she might become a fit bride for one of Redwald's nephews. Only the servant Gode knew of the bitter tears in the lonely apartment, when Hereswith's pallet was taken away.

It was not for nothing that Edwin had taught Hilda of her royal heritage, for though she scorned the trappings of nobility she had learned that a commanding presence and imperious ways would gain her will when those in authority would not take her seriously. Tall, straight and proud, she stood before Edwin now in answer to his summons, pleased to see him for he had been many weeks away occupying his restless warriors with forays to the west and making triumphal journeys through his territories in the Roman manner as he awaited news from Kent.

'How tall you grow!' he exclaimed, seeing with pleasure how noble she was in feature and bearing, how glowing with health and vigour, even if she was not beautiful. 'Truly a royal lady, and I hear from all sides of your good progress in the tasks assigned to you, and of your concern for all alike, both high and low. Yet you must remember that you are still a child, and curb your anger if you cannot always have your way. There are some that you sometimes offend.'

Hilda flushed and looked at him with clear grey eyes. 'I know it,' she said, 'but I am angry only with good cause.

Sometimes I see very clearly what is right, when others do not. But I will fight it,' she added obediently.

Edwin smiled and motioned her to sit down on a low stool at his side. As she did so the goats' hair mantle that covered her head and shoulders fell back and he saw that the thick braids of her light brown hair were unadorned, and that her undyed woollen tunic was of a coarser weave than he expected her to wear, and that its only decoration was the bronze needle case and double-sided comb of bone that hung from the girdle and the hooked bronze plates that fastened the braided cuffs.

'And are you still determined that you will not wear the royal gemstones and fine garments, even though you fast become a woman?' he enquired a little sternly.

'I ask you to forgive me,' she said. 'I go often among the poor people and would feel ill at ease if I wore fine clothing and jewels.'

'No-one would dare to rob you,' replied Edwin, 'for they know that they would die for it.'

'Indeed I know that they would never rob me,' exclaimed Hilda hotly, 'for I think that they love me, and that is not my reason. It is that it would make a gulf between me and the people that I do not wish. I beg that you will understand.' She looked at him pleadingly.

Edwin shrugged, for he did not understand, but he also saw that she needed no adornment to set her above others.

'I will not press it any more,' he said. 'And now I have a matter of great importance for you that you are among the first to hear, for it concerns you closely. Soon I will marry again. It is many years now since the death of the mother of my sons. Osfrid and Eadfrid are grown men and may fall in battle. I would have more heirs to the line of Woden. I will take as my wife Ethelburga, daughter of Ethelbert of Kent and sister to the present king, Eadbald, for she has grown fair and is come to marriageable age. Her mother was Bertha, daughter of the Frankish king Charibert, and so the court of Kent has much traffic with the land of the Franks whose shores are so close, and with the traders who travel its routes

27

to distant lands. Such connection would add greatly to my power and wealth.'

Edwin paused and looked at her. He did not disguise his ambition and Hilda understood perfectly the implications of such an alliance. She nodded in agreement and waited for him to continue.

'But,' he went on slowly, 'there are conditions to our union, for she is a Christian. I think you know something of this faith?'

'Very little,' replied Hilda, looking at him squarely for he knew very well that her enquiries into such matters had been discouraged. 'It has been difficult to find out about it. The high priest sends the monks away too quickly when they come. I think that my mother was deeply stirred by what she heard from the monk, Botulf. Gode has told me of her meeting with him. I think that she might have come to accept this faith, had she lived.'

'It may be that very soon you shall learn about it to your heart's content,' said Edwin. 'Eadbald has replied that it is not permissible for a Christian maiden to be given in marriage to a heathen husband, lest the Christian faith and sacraments be profaned by her association with a king wholly ignorant of the worship of the true God. Those are his words. But I am determined for this alliance, and so I have promised to place no obstacles in the way of the Christian faith and will afford complete freedom to Ethelberga and her attendants, both men and women, priests and servants, to live and worship in accordance with Christian belief and practice. And I have even said,' Edwin's eyes wavered before the clear expectant gaze, 'that I am willing to accept the religion of Christ, if, on examination, my advisors decide that it appears more holy and acceptable to God than our own. Ethelburga will bring with her as chaplain Paulinus, a man beloved of God it is said, and I know that it is her dearest wish, and that it will be Paulinus' mission also, encouraged by the Pope in Rome himself, that I should embrace this faith.'

He shifted uneasily in his carved chair and looked at her again. 'Yet the gods of our race have served me very well.

The sacrifices made by the high priest Coifi, have been followed by great victories, and he says that the vengeance of the gods would be great if I foreswore them and betrayed my forefather Woden.'

'Perhaps you need not trouble yourself about this yet,' said Hilda tactfully. 'But wait until you have learned more about the Christian God. You are a great and wise king and will give a just hearing to this teaching as well as to the words of Coifi.'

She scorned Coifi and did not trust him, thinking that he played upon Edwin's fears and fawned upon him, and that he was too much taken into the king's confidence. Besides he was dirty and unkempt and some of his rites disturbed her. She shrank from the sacrifice of animals, the cruel throat-cutting, the rituals with the blood that incited the people to unnatural ecstasy.

'I will indeed bring an open mind to the matter,' said Edwin, somewhat relieved. 'The court of Kent has my promise, and there is plenty of time.' He paused. 'There may be opportunity to test this God. If he would have me as a convert perhaps he will grant me a great victory first.'

But Hilda's thoughts had turned from such serious matters and childlike again she asked excitedly, 'Ethelburga is very young?'

'She is only a few years older than yourself,' he answered, 'and I hope that you will be good companions. For her it will mean great change, and loneliness, and you will help her to understand the ways of our court. For you it will lighten the sorrow of your parting with Hereswith. I know that this was grievous for you, but it had to be. We will receive Ethelburga at York, for the waves and the wind of Bamburgh might alarm her, and there is still much work being done at Yeavering. I would have you diligent in devising matters for her comfort and happiness.'

So Hilda looked forward with eager expectancy to the coming of the young queen, and shared in the lavish preparations that Edwin set in train so that his court would outshine that of Kent, and Ethelburga and her attendants

29

not think that they were coming to a land of savages, as those in the south appeared to expect.

Forest was cleared, so that the high earthwork that surrounded the royal township could be extended and wood provided to raise new buildings ready for so greatly increased a household. Orders for fine hangings went out to those experienced in weaving and dyeing and embroidery, and the king's stewards travelled throughout the kingdom seeking the finest pottery from the kilns and purchasing intricately designed silver and metal ware, for the people were highly skilled in these crafts. There was traffic too with traders who dealt in precious goods from distant lands, in ivory and gold, in silks and precious stones, and pottery more delicate in form and colour than could be found in Britain, for word travelled quickly among them of Edwin's preparations.

It was in the high summer of that year of AD 625 that the first baggage wagons arrived from Kent, and with them Ethelburga's women attendants and servants, and Hilda could scarcely contain her excitement. Constantly she interrupted her tasks and ran to the fortified entrance gates to see if messengers were in sight. At last a horseman galloped in to say that the young queen and her attendants were only a few miles behind him, and Edwin came to the gates finely arrayed, his standard-bearer and his thanes in war gear at his side. Lilla stood close, watchful in case an assassin from Cadwallon or from Penda should be hiding among the strangers. But his time had not yet come. Beyond them were drawn up the priests and chief counsellors and members of the royal household, Hilda on tiptoe among them, and a concourse of people from the township and from the farmsteads and villages that lay in the forest clearances beyond.

The queen travelled in a great leather-covered wagon drawn by horses, and Edwin himself stepped forward to lift her down. Hilda saw that she was indeed only a girl, slight and frail in form, but with a regal dignity as Edwin set her on her feet and she looked up trustingly into his face and then turned to acknowledge the cheers and applause that

30

broke out on all sides. Edwin began to lead her away, but she stayed him with a gentle hand.

'My lord,' she said, 'I would have Paulinus accompany us.'

'As you will,' said Edwin and looking up at the wagon he called loudly to Paulinus to come forth. A servant sprang forward to hold back the hanging and there stepped down a tall stooping figure in a black habit, and Hilda thought that never had she seen so strange and arresting a face. He was dark, but not in the manner of the swarthy Britons who worked as slaves or who sometimes came to treat with Edwin from their remaining western strongholds, for this man's ancestry lay somewhere in the warm lands of the Mediterranean. His hair, tonsured round the crown in the Roman manner, hung in black points about an ascetic face with thin hooked nose and deeply sunken burning eyes that he turned first upon Edwin and then upon the assembled people, at the same time raising his right hand high in a majestic act of blessing.

It was Paulinus, servant of God, and newly consecrated bishop. Paulinus who would one day convert all of Northumbria. Paulinus who would re-found the great see of York, second only to the see of Canterbury, as it has remained to this day. The gaunt dark figure followed close behind the royal couple to the palace, and all eyes were upon him.

There began to be great changes in the court. Ethelburga was reared in the just and far-seeing laws that her father Ethelbert had instituted for his people, and she began to introduce them in Northumbria. She belied her frail appearance with an iron determination to bring to effect the daunting tasks entrusted to her. Serious beyond her years she bore upon her slight shoulders the burden of converting Edwin, of bearing his children, of administering his court and being at his side, wearing the royal apparel with regal grace at all times of ceremony. It was small wonder that she soon learned to love Hilda for her ready laughter, and for her independence of thought and action as she strode about her self-appointed tasks.

'And you do not love to wear these gemstones?' she asked

31

the girl one day as they looked together at the royal hoard displayed before her by the king's treasurer, so that she might choose what she would wear for the evening's feasting.

'No,' said Hilda forthrightly, but looking at them too with delight. 'Yet they are very beautiful, and I love to see them upon you.' She laughed in admiration as the young queen held a golden filet against the fair braids of her hair.

'So what will you do when one day you come to marry a noble husband who will wish to adorn you?' said Ethelburga playfully. But Hilda at once became earnest.

'I will never do so,' she replied, 'for I must remain free. I begin to feel a calling that there is something that I must do, but what it is I do not yet know. It will be a sorrow to me not to bear children because I dearly love them, but there will be yours to share, and indeed I can scarcely wait for the little one to be born.' For Ethelburga was already pregnant.

'That is a great decision to take at so early an age,' the queen replied seriously. She had soon learned not to treat Hilda as a child.

Ethelburga also began to respect what she saw to be a unique intelligence in her young companion, a passion to learn, and a fearless pleasure in questioning the intimidating Paulinus whose daily instruction of the queen Hilda had asked if she might share.

'I wish that I could understand the Latin language as quickly as you do,' Ethelberga said to her after a wearying lesson with the bishop. 'In truth I find it very difficult and am quite content to abandon it. I shall ask Paulinus to spare me any more, and to continue our instruction in the faith without it. But he shall arrange for you to study it with one of the monks, for I see the pleasure that it brings you.'

So the light of Christianity began to dawn for Hilda and the gospels were opened to her eager understanding. The monks who accompanied Paulinus continued with their studies of the scriptures, and with the copying of the sacred texts that they had brought with them. There were learned scholars among them, and no one dared any longer forbid Hilda to question and learn from them all that she wished. But she

32

bided her time and did not ask for baptism, waiting and hoping that soon the time would come when Edwin would accept the faith and all his household receive it together gladly. But here seemed an insurmountable task indeed, and Hilda was amazed that so brave a man should show such craven fear and hover for so long upon the brink of faith. His young bride, who in everything else he most fondly indulged, could make no headway with him and nor could the scholarly Paulinus, who toiled unceasingly from the day that he arrived to convert not only the king but also his pagan subjects. Yet no one would listen, and all that the bishop could do was to maintain the faith of his own companions, by daily celebration of mass and religious instruction, against the corruption of their constant association with such a heathen race.

In the springtime of the following year Edwin moved a small part of his court to his country seat beside the river Derwent, there to await the birth of Ethelburga's child. Besides her women servants the queen had asked that Hilda, now her constant companion, should accompany her, nor would she stir without Paulinus although Edwin would have been better pleased had he stayed among his monks in York. And Lilla would not remain behind and came with a handful of loyal thanes to be always at the king's side.

On Easter day Paulinus celebrated the greatest of the Christian festivals with mass for Ethelburga and her companions. It was clear that the queen's time was very close and Hilda watched her tenderly. Towards evening Edwin returned from a hunting party to find that the young thane called Forthere, left to guard the queen, had admitted a messenger from Cuichelm, King of the West Saxons.

'The queen is not yet delivered,' the youth greeted Edwin, 'and there is a thane come with messages from Cuichelm. His name is Eumer, and he assured me that you knew him well, so I have allowed him to await you.'

The king shrugged, 'I do not recall him,' he said, 'but send him now quickly and then we can prepare for the feasting.'

So Edwin stood carelessly, his few thanes about him, anxious to be rid of the fellow who came now and knelt before him and began to deliver his message.

Red-headed Lilla stands close. Sees the man rise suddenly. Sees the flash of the long dagger hidden under his mantle. Sees with wonder his own entrails spill upon the floor as the dagger drives and twists. Clenches his teeth through his tongue so that no shriek will shame him. Knows his wish fulfilled, and sees no more. For having no shield he has flung his body before the king and died at last for the sons of Woden. Red locks in the dust. Red blood mingling with the blood of Woden, for Edwin falls wounded, pierced by the dagger through the body of his knight. Then the young thane, Forthere, leaps in savage anger upon the assassin, fearless of the dagger still in his hand, and dies upon its point before the man is attacked from all sides and slaughtered.

Edwin's wound was not deep, but bled profusely for the dagger was double-edged, and he was faint and sick by the time the flow was staunched. Yet when news was brought to him that night of the queen's safe delivery of a daughter, to be named Enfleda, he rallied and sent for all the court to stand about his couch to witness his thanksgiving to the gods. Then Paulinus, who was also present, stepped forward, and gently putting aside the high priest Coifi who stood beside the king to prompt him in the ritual words of thanksgiving, he knelt beside Edwin and took his hand between his own.

'I offer up thanks to Christ,' he said, 'for I have not ceased to pray for the queen's safe and painless delivery, and he has granted my prayer.'

Edwin looked into the aquiline face and saw there a passion of sincerity and love, and felt a strength returning through the touch of those hands.

'If God will grant me my life,' he said to Paulinus, 'and then victory when I take revenge upon the king my enemy, who dared to sent this assassin, then I will renounce my gods and serve your Christ, and as pledge that I will keep my word you may take my infant daughter and consecrate her

34

to Christ's service. She shall be the first among the Northumbrians to receive baptism. It will greatly please the queen,' he added. 'Tell her now and reassure her that I am recovering.'

He turned to his thanes, 'And now,' he said, 'prepare the body of the hero Lilla for burial. Bear him on his shield to the high ground that lies to the north east, between Derwent and the sea, and there bury him with every honour and set up a stone to mark the place for ever.'

'Let it be carved in the form of a cross my lord,' said Paulinus, 'that people may see it and know how the Lord has preserved your life on this day as well as the queen's.'

'Let it be so,' said Edwin.

The king kept his promise and on the Feast of Pentecost Paulinus took the infant Enfleda into his arms and baptised her into the Christian faith, and twelve others from the queen's family and household received baptism at the same time. Yet still Hilda waited, sure though she was in the faith, because of her love and loyalty to Edwin.

The king's recovery took some time, for the dagger had been poisoned, but as soon as he was fully recovered he called his battle-hungry thanes to arms and wreaked bloody vengeance upon the West Saxons. His victory was celebrated with triumph, with feasting and song and display of arms, with adulation that was close to worship for the mighty son of Woden, with gifts and rewards for his brave warriors. But the son of Woden was thrown into turmoil, for how could he now renounce his sacred ancestry and the loyalty and beliefs of his people, the brave acts of war and the ceremony that bound them to him and that were so dear to his own heart too? And the high priest Coifi stood in the shadows, watching the gift-giving with envy, whispering of the vengeance of the gods into the king's ear, for Edwin had already renounced the idols of his race to please Paulinus and would no longer permit sacrifice to them. The king brooded for a long time upon the matter and at last decided what he should do.

'You shall give me a full course of instruction in the faith,' he said to Paulinus, 'before I can accept baptism. Some of

35

my chief counsellors, whose wisdom I greatly respect and rely on, shall attend too, and then in due time I can discuss my proper course in council with them.'

So the matter went on being deferred. Patiently Paulinus instructed Edwin, and Ethelburga gently and firmly encouraged him. At the same time the king received a letter from Rome from Pope Boniface, who had heard of the difficulty that Paulinus was encountering in Northumbria. It urged him, with powerful argument, to accept the faith, and Boniface sent very precious gifts, a garment with a golden ornament and a robe from Ancyra, that greatly moved the king. By the same messengers he also sent word to Ethelburga bidding her renew her efforts for the king's salvation, and there were gifts for her too, a silver mirror and a comb wrought in gold and ivory that filled her with delight, although she was at her wits end as to how to persuade Edwin.

Paulinus was close now in the king's councils and trusted by those about him, even though he could not convert them, and so he learned from one close to Edwin of the vision that had come to him while he was an exile at Redwald's court before his victory over Ethelfrith, and of the promise that he had given to the man in his dream that he would faithfully follow the guidance of anyone who should one day give him the same sign again, and place his right hand upon his head. So Paulinus went to find the king who was sitting alone lost in thought, as was so often now his habit, and laying his right hand upon Edwin's head asked him whether he remembered the sign.

Never was such subtlety so justified. Edwin's last doubts dissolved before so sure a sign. He paled and trembled and made to abase himself. Paulinus raised him, bid him at once accept the faith, and promised that his obedience would save him from the everlasting doom of the wicked and gain him a place in God's eternal kingdom.

It only remained for Edwin to call his council and gain their agreement, so that they might all be saved together, and the people more readily abide by the decision. And he

36

need not have feared his high priest, and the wrath of the ancient gods. Coifi capitulated with the greatest of ease. He rounded upon the gods for their injustice to himself, who had never gained the favours and rewards received by others far less devoted to their service. The next of the king's counsellors nodded his agreement with this prudent argument:

'Your Majesty,' he said, 'when we compare the present life of man with that time of which we have no knowledge, it seems to me like the swift flight of a lone sparrow through the banqueting-hall where you sit in the winter months to dine with your thanes and counsellors. Inside there is a comforting fire to warm the room; outside, the wintry storms of snow and rain are raging. This sparrow flies swiftly in through one door of the hall, and out through another. While he is inside, he is safe from the winter storms; but after a few moments of comfort, he vanishes from sight into the darkness whence he came. Similarly, man appears on earth for a little while, but we know nothing of what went before this life, and what follows. Therefore if this new teaching can reveal any more certain knowledge, it seems only right that we should follow it.'

With this the whole council signified agreement, and indeed, after asking some instruction from Paulinus, Coifi became as zealous for the new teaching as he had once been for the old. He publicly confessed his faith in it and vowed that for long he had searched diligently, but in vain, for any truth in the religion of his people. Further, he suggested to Edwin that the ancient shrines should be desecrated and burned, volunteering for the task himself so that he might make public example of his former ignorance by profaning the temples and idols that he had himself dedicated and served. So great was his enthusiasm that he asked of the king arms and a stallion, hitherto forbidden to the priestly order, and so girded he rode East from York to the shrine of Goodmanham beyond the river Derwent. The crowd who followed held their breath in amazement, thinking him out of his wits, sure that he would be tossed, and Hilda, watching

37

discreetly from afar, spluttered with unseemly laughter. But the priest arrived without mishap and joyfully cast his spear into the temple to profane it, and bid his companions burn it to the ground together with the enclosures that surrounded it.

Upon Easter Day, the twelfth day of April in the year AD 627, King Edwin was baptised by Paulinus. The ceremony took place at York, in the church of St Peter the Apostle, newly built for the purpose upon an open space within the ruins of the Roman city. The nobles of Edwin's court kneeled too before the bishop to be touched by the cleansing water, and among them the thirteen-year-old Hilda joyfully received at last the sign of the cross upon her forehead. Very many too of Edwin's humbler subjects followed his example, and in the years that followed his sons Osfrid and Eadfrid were baptised, and the children born to Ethelburga, and Iffi, the infant son of Osfrid, so that all the royal family was Christian.

Then Edwin established the see of York with Paulinus as its bishop, and soon he sent to Gaul for masons who were skilled in the art of building in stone. They began work on a noble stone basilica to replace, upon the same site, the earlier small wooden church that had been erected for Edwin's baptism.

And now the fervour of faith began to spread like fire throughout Northumbria. Paulinus accompanied the king and queen to their capital at Yeavering, and for thirty-six days, from dawn till dusk, he preached to the northern tribes of Bernicia. From the villages and countryside they flocked to hear his words in the great amphitheatre at Yeavering that Edwin had built, in the style of ancient Rome, as a gathering place for his people. And because there had not been time yet to build churches he baptised his northern converts in the waters of the river Glen that runs close to Yeavering, and those from Deira in the river Swale that flows near the village of Catterick.

Edwin was now determined that the faith should shine into every corner of the land where he had influence, and Paulinus made more converts in the province of Lindsey, which lay to the south of Deira, where Edwin was overlord. He was assisted there in his missionary work by James, a deacon of great energy and repute in the church, and together they baptised the people in the River Trent. And in the city of Lincoln a great stone church was built, and it was there that Paulinus consecrated Honorius as Archbishop of Canterbury, a ceremony which as bishop of York and next in seniority he had the authority to perform.

And at this time news of Paulinus' success at last, with Edwin, reached the Pope in Rome. He wrote letters to Edwin and to Paulinus; and to the Archbishop of Canterbury he dispatched the pallium, that is the woollen vestment that signifies the office of Archbishop, so that in his turn Honorius could confer it upon Paulinus for the see of York.

Next Edwin looked to East Anglia and at last persuaded its king, Eorpwald, who was Redwald's son, to abandon the idols that he worshipped and receive the faith that his father had so half-heartedly embraced for fear of his queen. This brought great joy to Hilda's sister, Hereswith, for she could just remember encountering the monk Botulf as a child. Like Hilda she had yearned to learn more of the faith, but had not dared for fear of Redwald's queen, now dead. But the queen's memory still held sway among the East Anglian people, and King Eorpwald died at the hand of a pagan assassin for his betrayal of the gods of their race. His brother, the Christian prince Sigbert, exiled to France for his belief, returned to succeed him. He brought with him greetings to Hereswith from Botulf, now a venerated teacher in the monastery at Chelles, for the monk had always nursed the hope that the daughters of Bregusyth might one day join him there as nuns.

In the year AD 630, the Irish Abbot Fursey came to East Anglia with some companions. Sigbert gave them the ancient fortress that is now called Burgh Castle with its adjacent lands, for a monastery, so that they could carry out missionary work among his people. The king worked devotedly to this end himself and he was ably assisted by the bishop Felix, appointed by Archbishop Honorius to a new episcopal see at Dunwich, on the coast of Lindsey.

To the north and west of Northumbria, Christianity had been established in some degree among the Britons ever since the time of the Romans, and later it was reinforced by missionaries from those independent monasteries and cells founded in the far west long before Augustine came to Kent, upon very ancient traditions. Among the native British people Christianity was already strong.

So it seemed that with the conversion of Northumbria a great part of Britain burned with the growing faith. But as the first gales of autumn raged in the year AD 632, the flame in Edwin's kingdom was blown out.

40

CHAPTER 4

ilda was sitting with Ethelburga in the women's quarters of the palace at York listening to the wind wailing through the great trees of the forest. It was the evening of the twelfth day of October in the year AD 632 and the winds of the autumn equinox were blowing early. Their eyes stung from the smoke that was forced back through the vent in the thatched roof to billow through the curtained apartments, and they spoke together in hushed tones, for the six-year-old Enfleda was asleep, snug beneath the rich coverings of her small pallet. Ethelburga nursed at her breast the infant prince Wuscfrea, and Hilda watched them fondly for she knew the joy that this child brought to the queen; joy that she had born Edwin a son, and comfort in her desolation for the two children who had died in infancy.

The two young women did not hide their anxiety from one another. There had been no respite from it since Edwin had armed his forces in haste and ridden against the British king Cadwallon, risen in rebellion from Gwynedd and thrusting across the country unopposed to reach the borders of Northumbria. Now news had come that Penda of Mercia had grasped the opportunity to overthrow Edwin at last, and that his forces were marching to join the British against him.

'I pleaded with Edwin not to go on this campaign,' said Ethelburga, 'but to treat for peace with Cadwallon and find some settlement honourable to them both. But the warrior-god is strong within him still, and his thanes still thirst for the glory of battle. Besides, he can never forgive his enemies for the death of Osfrid in the last skirmish. It is hard for him

41

not to seek revenge. And he believes that God will grant him victory. But I have grave and bitter fears of these latest tidings concerning Penda. Edwin thought him safely occupied with raids into East Anglia and no great threat.'

'There has been plotting, and treachery,' said Hilda, 'but messengers should be here soon now to tell us how the battle fares, for it was said that Edwin is close to Doncaster and that is no great distance for a horseman to come with tidings. Perhaps Edwin himself may come soon,' she added, attempting to offer a comfort that she did not feel.

'Only if he is victor,' said Ethelburga in a low voice.

Now they fall silent and listen to the howling of the gale. And in a corner of the apartment the servant Gode shivers in fear. For there is whisper of evil portents, of grey wolf and black raven seen haunting the field of battle.

The howling of the gale grows louder and there begins to be another sound within it, a sound that is scarcely heard at first but that grows more insistent so that at the same moment the women raise their heads startled, and jump in alarm to their feet, Ethelburga still clasping the hungry child to her breast. For now the sound is clear. It is the people of the township wailing outside the palace, and their cry taken up by those within.

'Edwin! Edwin! Woe! Woe! Edwin the King is slain!'

There is weeping and moaning, and men shouting, and clatter of arms thrown down, and wind and billowing smoke as the outer doors are flung open and the young thane called Bassus bursts without ceremony into the apartment where the women crouch in foreboding. His garments are blood stained and rent and he looks ready to fall from exhaustion. The queen sinks near fainting upon a chair and he flings himself onto his knees before her, tears of grief for his lord furrowing the bloody grime upon his face.

'My lady,' he cries, 'Edwin is slain at Hatfield Chase and Eadfrid has surrendered to Penda and the whole army is slaughtered or fled. I live myself only because the king commanded me, when he saw that all would be lost, to leave the battle and ride at once to rescue you and the royal children, for his enemies will have no mercy for his heirs, or for yourself who may already carry another prince within your womb. We must fly at once, within the hour, and escape unseen while all is darkness and confusion still. I will escort you safe to Kent, and Paulinus shall come too to give you strength and comfort. I have made provision for us to hide with one that I can trust, near to the mouth of the Humber, for when the gale is spent we must take ship. To venture by land would mean certain death, for treachery is everywhere.' He looked at Hilda who stood with one arm supporting the queen, the other clasped about the child Enfleda, woken by the noise and clinging to her, white and terrified into silence.

'Prepare them speedily,' he said to her. 'Osfrid's son, the child Iffi, is being fetched for we must take him too. I go to seek Paulinus and to make provision,' he paused, 'we could take one other. You may accompany the queen.' He did not wait for her reply but went out in haste.

The queen recovered herself a little and stood in frozen silence while the servants wrapped her in furs and warmly clad the little girl and the infant princes, for Osfrid's son was quickly brought. She could not trust herself to speak but her eyes were fixed on Hilda in mute appeal, and Hilda clasped her hands in agony of doubt.

'I do not know what to do,' she cried. 'I must have time to think and to pray. I cannot leave now, at once. I must have this night to know God's will. Bassus shall tell me where you are going, so that I can follow. You know that you can trust me, but he must tell no-one else. I could quickly join you in a day or two, before you sail. But do not endanger your lives by waiting, for if I come it will be near at once. I cannot tell what to do,' she cried again. 'For indeed I wish to be with you and the children always, and yet I think our people here will need me in the days that lie ahead.'

'You will be in danger, Hilda,' Ethelburga managed to say in a trembling voice.

'My life means nothing to me now,' replied the girl bitterly, 'but still there is much that I could do with it, and I think you need not fear for me. I am far from the succession to

Edwin. His kinsman Osric is at hand, and there are the sons of Ethelfrith. I think the enemy will not harm me.' She raised her head bravely.

Then Paulinus came and knelt quickly beside the queen to comfort her and to whisper that he had secured some of Edwin's treasures, among them the golden cross and chalice hallowed for use at the altar, but she was too distraught to understand and only bowed her head silently.

Soon Bassus returned. He did not press Hilda to come with them, but whispered their destination to her. Paulinus, seeing her mind made up, placed his hand upon her head in blessing.

'You are brave and wise,' he said, 'and will come to a right decision. You will give the people courage and guidance if you do remain. It grieves me bitterly to leave the work of conversion here, and I shall never now receive the pallium. But my place is at the queen's side, and I must trust my work to James the deacon.'

Then Bassus and a servant carried away the children and Paulinus led Ethelburga out into the noise and darkness.

All night Hilda struggled to know her right course. Dearly she loved Ethelburga and her children, and she knew that should she go to Kent there would be work that she could do among its people. But she loved the Northumbrian people and knew that dark and terrible days lay ahead for them. All night she lay in a passion of tears. Tears for Edwin who had been a father to her. Tears for Ethelburga and the little children, set out upon so dangerous a journey. Tears for all mankind who must cause one another such suffering. Tears for herself, lonely and afraid. And all night the faithful Gode sat beside her, moaning to herself, calling upon the ancient gods for help although she had been baptised a Christian.

Then Hilda knew, knew what she must do. If Gode was helpless and so easily lost faith then so would others, and what would happen to Edwin's people whom it had always been her care to love and serve? She would stay.

Weak and sick from the struggle to reach a decision and

from the sorrow of the night, she rose in the bleak first light and went out to find those most in need.

No more than a handful had returned from the battle, and those only to give what tidings they could before leaving again in haste to find hiding. The slain lay where they had fallen, plundered of their war-gear, to be buried on the battle field. The wounded had been slaughtered, and the rest captured or fled into exile.

There was silence in the royal township, silence and deep dread as the people awaited the coming of the conquerors.

But the conquerors did not come yet. They had suffered heavy losses themselves and must re-gather their forces. There was uneasy peace. Edwin's severed head was brought in ceremony to the church of St Peter that he had begun to build in York. There it rested in the porch that was newly dedicated to Pope Gregory, and the people flocked to venerate it. But Hilda sickened at the thought and would not go.

Northumbria fell back into its divided kingdoms. Osric, cousin to Edwin, claimed Deira, and Eanfrid, nephew to Edwin and eldest of the sons of Ethelfrith, seized his chance and returned from exile as rightful heir to Bernicia. It seemed then that the work of Paulinus would continue, for both were Christian: Osric baptised by Paulinus, and Eanfrid brought up in the faith by the monks of the island monastry of Iona that was founded by the holy Columba. Yet the people lost heart and began turning back to the old gods, angry that the Christian god had not brought victory. Then the two princes, Osric and Eanfrid, finding themselves the inheritors of rich kingdoms, also abandoned the Christian faith and returned to the pagan traditions of their ancestors. James the deacon could make no headway, and the monks of Paulinus began to scatter and to make their way back to the south.

Hilda grieved deeply that the people, converted in such numbers and with such seeming conviction, could so quickly fall back into their old ways. Yet it did not go unheeded among them that she herself would not do so but continued to receive mass and daily instruction from the monks who remained, and that she never ceased her care for the poor and outcast and gave glad assistance to Osric's royal household in the ways of the court that she understood so well. But she grew weary and discouraged, and prey to anxiety for no news had reached her yet of Ethelburga and Paulinus, and pains in the stomach began to trouble her. James the deacon, visiting the court at York one day from his dwelling near Catterick to bring her news that he had just received, was startled by the change he saw in her.

'I bring good news, Lady Hilda,' he said, observing her closely. 'A monk has made his way to me from the household that sheltered Ethelburga and Paulinus after they fled with Bassus. They remained there hidden for many days until the storm abated and then they embarked from the estuary of the Humber. The monk watched from the shore as their vessel was carried out of sight by strong oarsmen helped by a sail set to catch a fair wind that sprang up. The wind has continued many days and the weather has been mild and I think that already they may be safe in Kent.'

He saw some colour return to her cheeks and the grey eyes light up.

'What joy you bring me,' she cried, 'to know that they may be safe. It is all that I care about. Although I think I may never see them again in this life,' she added sombrely.

'No', he said, 'for I believe that Ethelburga will take the veil and seek peace in the holy life of a monastery. The little princes will not be safe even in Kent from Edwin's enemies, and I think must be taken from her and sent to her kinsman, Dagobert, in Gaul. Perhaps Enfleda will one day return to us,' he tried to cheer her, seeing her downcast again. But she was thinking of other matters, and raising her head she asked him bitterly,

'How can the people lose their faith so readily, and even Osric and Eanfrid apostatise? How can it be, after all that Paulinus did; his instructions in the scriptures and in the fathers, his powerful exhortation, and your own patient teaching?'

'For some perhaps conversion came too readily,' replied James, 'without sufficient thought, so that the light of faith flared with too bright a flame, a fire with no depth that has flickered and gone out. I have known it happen so before, after the mass baptisms when all have been caught up by Paulinus' eloquence and the ecstasy of those about them. Faith that endures comes slowly, after much searching and understanding of the scriptures. It has always been so, since the days of the first disciples. Have no fear, Christianity cannot die out. The people will be shown the way again, they will learn from those like yourself whose faith is unshaken by adversity, and from the holy example and teaching of the monks who have remained. As for their present leaders, they are straws in the wind.'

She looked at him with earnest childlike gaze, drawing comfort from his words, and he was filled with compassion for her, struck by how young she was, and how alone.

'How old are you?' he asked.

'I am eighteen years old,' she answered, drawing herself up.

'I had always thought you more,' he said, 'nearer in age to the queen. It is because you undertake so many tasks among the people and have learned to shoulder suffering since you were a little child. You must have a care for yourself. What can I do to help you?'

'Ah,' cried Hilda, feeling strength and courage returning, 'how I would love to continue the studies that I started under Paulinus and his scholars, in the Latin tongue and in the scriptures. Are there any left who would instruct me?'

'I will find some,' said James, 'and will undertake to teach you when I can myself.'

'When my own understanding is improved,' she said eagerly, 'I can explain the scriptures to the people in our own tongue.'

'Yes,' he answered, 'and there are other ways to teach them. If you come to the church of St Peter you shall hear singing of great beauty. I have found among the monks, and among some of the lay people, those who have received from God the gift of music, and I am instructing them in the chants that I learned before I left Rome to come to Kent, and that we started to use in Canterbury. We have one who plays the lyre, and others whose voices I am training so that they blend like the heavenly choirs of the angels. It is a way to bring truth that cannot be expressed in the words of any language into the hearts of those who hear it. Then there are those who can carve in stone and wood, under whose hands the hard substance melts into images that will bring the scriptures and their meaning into the understanding of the unlettered. Pope Gregory himself advised the use of such carvings, and of paintings too, so that those who are ignorant of letters may at least read with their eyes upon the walls what they cannot read in books. Such art is an inspiration to the scholar too, enabling fresh insights.' He smiled at her and rose to go, 'You will find joy and comfort in this yourself,' he said.

'Indeed,' she cried, her face glowing, 'and we must seek out and encourage those who have these gifts. There are some that I know of already, among the people.'

So James left her much recovered, and she grew robust again and ready to face what lay ahead.

Then the dark days came. Eadfrid was treacherously murdered at Penda's court, and Osric and his forces destroyed by Cadwallon in a rash attempt that they made to beseige him in his stronghold. Finally Eanfrid too was slain, for he foolishly thought Cadwallon to be trusted and went unprotected to treat with him for peace.

For a year Cadwallon ruled Northumbria with ruthless savagery, sparing neither women nor children in his revenge upon the Anglo-Saxon kingdom, and in desperation the people implored the pagan gods to return and save them.

The British king called himself a Christian but he had no respect for the usages of Canterbury, and Paulinus' monks went in fear. But Hilda went in safety despite her faith and her royal blood, for the British slaves, freed now by the conquerors, spoke of her impartial compassion and justice, and would not see her harmed.

But Gode they killed, round-faced Gode, captured for their sport by a wandering war-band, who laughed at her for lying when she vowed herself British. Merry on mead they raped her and slew her.

Afterwards Hilda felt ill, sick with anguish. But with an effort she regained her strength, so that she might herself arrange a fitting burial.

'Gode shall have Christian burial,' she said to those about her, 'but there shall be the rites that she loved. She shall have music and dance and song.'

Then Gode was borne to her grave in the deep-dug soil of her ancestors and the people followed behind with ancient chanting, dancing with slow movement to a solemn measure that throbbed from drum and horn and lyre. And the monk who spoke the burial service did not demur, although he looked surprised, for James the deacon had said that these customs were to be permitted.

Hiding in the far north-west, in the mountain regions of the Pictish people, Oswald was waiting. Oswald was the second of the heirs of Ethelfrith, and of a very different nature from his brother Eanfrid. He was a brave warrior, but one who did not seek his own gain. He was a devout Christian, educated and baptised by the monks of Iona.

The Picts were a wild and ancient race, but among them were settlements made by races who had come from the kingdom of Dalriada on the north-east coast of Ireland. They became firmly established among the Pictish people and began to be known as the Scots. To these settlements Columba's monks, and the great saint himself before his death in the year AD 597, had journeyed from Iona to convert their Irish kinsfolk. Sheltered by them Oswald bided his time, receiving news from those of Edwin's warriors who were still in hiding, watching for his opportunity to seize and re-united Northumbria.

At last he set out with a small army of warriors, handpicked for their courage and for the strength of their faith in Christ. Marching secretly they passed undetected across the ruined ramparts of the great wall left by the Romans, that spans the country from Solway to Tyne. Arriving at the wild moorland and forested valleys that lie to its south in the neighbourhood of Hexham, they hid in dense woodland beside the brook of Denis, knowing from their spies that soon Cadwallon and his forces would pass along the highway that served the region.

When the sentries stationed on the hilltops reported that the British were mustering, and moving towards them along the highway to Carlisle, Oswald prepared for battle, but first he gave orders for a rough wooden cross to be made and a trench dug so that it might stand upright on the battle field. He himself held it in position while his men threw back the soil and pressed it down. Then he shouted the war cry to his waiting warriors.

'But first,' he cried to them, 'let us kneel together, and ask the true and living God Almighty of his mercy to protect us from the arrogant savagery of our enemies, since he knows that we fight in a just cause to save our nation.'

So the whole army knelt in prayer before advancing in the first light of dawn to take Cadwallon's superior forces by surprise. Attacking from the forested hills on every side, Oswald's men slew the British king and scattered his army.

The field of the battle was called Heavenfield, and Oswald's cross became venerated by the people for it was said that miracles were performed there, and that there was healing power in splinters taken from its wood.

It was in the year AD 634 that Oswald came in triumph to restore Northumbria.

It is the year that Cuthbert is born.

It is the year that Wilfrid is born.

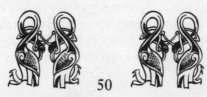

50

CHAPTER 5

Oswald quickly established law and order in Northumbria. The people were thankful for a ruler who they saw to be wise and just, as well as a royal prince and nephew to Edwin, and a great warrior too. But he was disturbed by the obdurate paganism of his subjects, particularly in his own province of Bernicia where Paulinus' preaching had made less impact than in Deira, and where there were still no churches. So he sent at once to the elders of the Scottish church for a bishop to preach to his people and to administer the sacraments. The bishop they chose first was an austere man whose name was Corman. He was angry with the people for their stubborness and threatened them with the wrath of God if they did not repent. They refused to listen to him and clung in fear to the gods that they understood. He returned to his superiors and reported that nothing could be done for so barbarous a race. But the Scots fathers knew of Oswald's determination, and also that there were still some among the Northumbrians who held to Christianity and longed for its return, and they summoned a conference to discuss the matter. Present at the conference was Aidan; Aidan, priest of God, trained in the tradition of Columba at the monastery of Iona, Aidan, scholar and ascetic, but a man of compassion, of gentleness and moderation.

Aidan addressed the discouraged Corman in no uncertain terms:

'Brother,' he said, 'it seems to me that you were too severe on your ignorant hearers. You should have followed the practice of the Apostles, and begun by giving them the milk of simpler teaching and gradually instructed them in the

51

word of God until they were capable of greater perfection and able to follow the sublime precepts of Christ.'

It was clear at once to everyone that Aidan himself was the man to go as bishop to the pagan Anglo-Saxons.

In the year AD 635 Aidan was consecrated and began his mission to Northumbria. For the principle monastery of his see he requested from the king the lonely island of Lindisfarne, whose desolate peninsula thrusts into the silver North Sea tideways, that twice daily flood its causeway to the mainland. Close to it was the royal stronghold, built upon the cliff of Bamburgh, where Oswald had set up his court.

Quickly the people came to love Aidan, for he went amongst them as one of themselves, refusing even the use of a horse so that he might not appear to stoop to them. Living as the poorest, seeking nothing for himself, he showed them the monastic way of prayer and study and asceticism. In his missionary work he was soon joined by other Scottish monks, and he was assisted by Oswald himself who not only gave generously of both wealth and land for establishing monasteries but also helped to interpret for his bishop from the Irish tongue, until Aidan had mastered the Anglo-Saxon language.

Those Christians who had retained the faith taught them by Paulinus began to notice that there were differences between the customs that had developed in the Scottish (that is to say, the Irish) church, and the canons of Rome that they had learned from the churchmen of Kent. To some these differences were disturbing and raised questions about the validity of their faith, but to others they seemed unimportant because the consecration of the Irish bishops and clergy through the laying on of hands still followed the apostolic succession from the apostle Peter. And the canons of scripture and the liturgy laid down by the early fathers at the first councils of the Church were faithfully followed.

James the deacon, deeply involved now in establishing the new stonebuilt church of St Peter in York, and in training its choir, mused on these questions with Hilda as they ended one of his promised lessons in Latin. For Hilda had chosen to remain in York following Oswald's accession, partly to assist him in the administration of the southern province, but also that she might continue the studies that she had started there.

'I do not think that matters such as the accurate dating of Easter are of very great importance,' James said. 'In all the essentials these Scottish monks are in agreement with us, and their scholarship in the scriptures and in the fathers is of the highest order. They have had to adapt to the needs of the remote tribes whom they serve, and to their own traditions of monasticism that started in the very century of our Lord's life. For it was then that some of the first Christians fled from the persecutions in Rome and from the conflicts of doctrine that were already besetting the early Church, and found refuge as anchorites in the Mediterranean deserts. But in the south of Ireland, so they tell me, customs have been closer to the canons of Rome, and the clergy there have now agreed to use the Roman calendar. The holy Patrick was a Roman Briton and studied for his orders on the continent after his escape from slavery in Ireland, so that it was in the Roman tradition that he taught the southern Irish people when he returned to them as a missionary. In the ancient church of the Britons, founded in the earliest days of the Roman conquest, customs vary again. But there is concern now about these differences in high places, and the Pope has written from Rome to the Scots and warned them that they must not stand apart from the rest of Christendom. In too great an independence lie the seeds of heresy, such as the British church has already suffered.'

Hilda was thoughtful. 'Perhaps one day when the whole country is converted, and the Church growing in other countries too, a common rule will become essential for proper administration,' she said, for she had a passion for sound organisation. 'But how I have come to love and respect these Irish monks, who live themselves exactly as they teach that others should. The monastic rules appeal to me very much, and one day I shall live by such a rule myself.'

James smiled at her with great affection. 'There is plenty

53

of time,' he said, 'as yet you are too much needed in secular activities. Oswald could not do without your experience in matters of justice and administration and leaves much in your hands.'

'How blessed we are now,' cried Hilda, 'after those terrible days, to have a ruler such as Oswald, and Oswin as lord of Deira who does not seek to rival the king but rules in accord with him, and shares his piety.'

James noticed with interest how she flushed at the name of the young prince, Osric's son, who held the southern province under Oswald.

'I think God's kingdom is already coming,' she cried, 'when princes begin to live in accord with one another. Do you not think so?'

She looked at him expectantly but he answered her sombrely,

'These good times and good people serve as a revelation to us, a vision of what can be, that we can hold on to when evil times come again, as they will until the ending of the world.'

He looked away from her bright face. He did not wish to remind her of the constant threat from Penda, or that Oswald's brother Oswy, waiting impatiently to succeed him, was full of worldly ambition although he was a Christian. Then he turned to her again to enquire if she had yet had any opportunity for discourse with the bishop, Aidan.

'He feels strongly that women must take part in the life of the Church,' he said, 'and that those of them who feel called to serve it must fulfil that calling.'

'That is so,' replied Hilda, 'for he has observed how Oswald's sister, the lady Ebba, abbess now of Coldingham where she was for some time a nun, conducts her monastery so wisely, and he has appointed the Lady Hieu as abbess of Hartlepool. I have not yet spoken to Aidan but Oswald wishes me soon to visit Coldingham, and that is not far from Lindisfarne. I hope that I can visit Aidan then and that he will grant me the time to tell me about Iona and all that he knows of the holy Columba, who rules still from his grave though forty years have gone by since he died, so greatly do his monks love his memory and the wisdom of his rule.'

The abbess Ebba, educated with her brothers in exile in Iona, brought royal endowment to the double monastery at Coldingham, which stood above the sea near the northern border of Bernicia. Here monks and nuns, their quarters separated from one another in different parts of the monastic enclosure, joined together in corporate worship, study, and toil. Ebba was much occupied in extending the monastery and establishing her rule, in which she was free to use her own discretion, when Hilda visited her in the spring of the following year.

Ebba saw at once the younger woman's great aptitude for adminstration, as well as in learning, and she lost no time in sending a messenger to Aidan to say that they would shortly visit him, and together they set out one day for the royal palace at Bamburgh. Oswald had lent them strong horses and insisted that servants accompany them, for they were royal ladies, though Hilda would rather have ridden alone for she knew the tracks that skirted the Cheviots and followed the coast from childhood days when Edwin's court had moved between the strongholds of Yeavering and Bamburgh, and she was a fearless horsewoman. The weather was mild and clear after the long and bitter winter, and waves of energy and delight surged through her as she moved in unison with the animal beneath her. Ebba glanced in admiration at the tall commanding figure; one of the daughters of Woden, surely, who galloped the skies in the sagas that were told by the wandering bards. They lodged that night in the royal palace, so that they would be ready to cross the natural causeway to Lindisfarne as soon as the tide had fallen enough the next morning.

The day was warm when they crossed to the island the following day. The sea was still and the colour of pearl in the pale sun, turning to cream where it lapped the sand. Laughing they splashed through the receding pools and sprang nimbly from rock to rock, holding up their cumbersome garments. The gentle breeze carried fresh scents of sea-wrack, and of new vegetation and the herbs that the monks were planting in the sheltered parts of the island. Sea-birds swooped to find food for their nestlings on the cliffs, and in the distance the light glinted from the shining heads of seals that bobbed among the sea-washed rocks.

At the end of the causeway a spare figure stood with arms outstretched to greet them. Nothing distinguished Aidan from the monks about him for he wore the same poor habit of undyed woollen cloth, threadbare from long wear and toil and girdled with a leather thong, and a rough wooden cross hanging upon his breast. But as they approached more closely Hilda knew that it was him, from the quiet authority of his gentle bearing and the compassion that shone from the eyes beneath the wide intelligent brow framed by the tonsured band of thick grey hair. She wanted to kneel at his feet but knew that he would not wish it.

'A jewel of a day,' he called out to them in the Irish tongue, and Hilda turned questioningly to Ebba for she did not yet understand it, then nodded to him in vigorous agreement.

He led them from the beach and through the new settlement where monks and lay brothers were labouring and had already erected cells of wood and wattle, at present housing the workforce. He showed them where the refectory and kitchen would lie, and the infirmary and more cells for the monks, and then the foundations for a scriptorium, because he wished Lindisfarne to be an important centre for the copying of sacred texts. Already monks skilled in this art were making their way there from the monasteries that Columba had founded; from Iona, and from Kells and Durrow in Ireland.

'There must be as much light as possible,' Aidan told them, 'you will see that there are to be wide apertures, for the finest work can only be done in daylight. And see the spaces marked for great hearths down the centre of the building. The monks cannot work with cold hands and the ink must flow smoothly.' He smiled, 'It is a popular place in the winter.'

Beside the scriptorium there would be a jewellers's workshop, he explained, for the designs of fine filigree used in metalwork could be adapted for the decorated pages of the manuscripts. It would be a profitable industry, too, so close to the royal court, and would help in relieving the needs of the poor.

Then they came to the church, which was near completion, with the thatchers at work on the roof. And then the bell sounded for the office of Sext, and everyone left their labour and joined in the service. There was no problem with language because the form and the Latin responses were common to them all. And next they joined in the main meal of the day, a soup of vegetables thickened with grain, freshly caught fish, and bread, and clear spring water; Hilda was considerably relieved that it was not a fast day.

Ebba then asked if she could look again at the layout of the monastery and discuss the problems of building with the monks who were directing it. There was so much that she could learn from them, and she also wished Aidan to have some time alone with Hilda. It was Aidan's policy to take a number of Anglo-Saxon boys into the monastery for training, and one of these youths, who had quickly picked up the Irish tongue of his teachers, was sent for to act as interpreter for him.

Hilda turned to the bishop, her face alight with energy and eagerness, 'Your time is very precious,' she said, 'but how I long to know about Iona, about holy Columba, and about your understanding of the Christian faith that in certain ways seems different to that taught me by Paulinus.'

'Ours is a monastic organisation,' he said, 'whereas the Roman canon has developed to meet the needs of the larger populations found in cities, such as we do not have in these islands. The dating of our calendar derives from a different and more ancient tradition. I do not intend to change it, and the king is in full agreement with me.' He spoke with quiet authority. 'You will understand the differences and how they have come about as you study the fathers and the first councils of the church, where the foundations of its laws and liturgy were laid and the canons of scripture chosen. You will have seen that our observance of the services is very much the same. These things may matter more as the church grows, but are of little importance compared with the study of the scriptures and a striving to follow a pattern of living as near as is possible to that of our Lord. This was the life that Columba followed, and that is why his memory lives on. I never knew him, for I was an infant at the time of his death and entered the monastery of Iona as a youth. But there were many then that remembered him, and some still remain among the monks who love to talk about him and tell stories of his compassion and humility, and of the simple and Christ-like life that he lived.'

'He came to Iona from Ireland?' asked Hilda.

'He was a royal prince of Dalriada,' replied the bishop, 'a warrior of great strength and commanding presence, but also a fine scholar, for you will know that there is advanced scholarship in the monasteries of Ireland. He was a poet, and deeply devout, but a man of passion who was sometimes, in his youth, both harsh and obstinate. Indeed it is said that his journey to Iona with his twelve companions was an exile, a punishment because he refused to give up a psalter that he had copied for his own use, and that the court that was called to resolve the issue claimed was the property of the monastery that held the manuscript. But I believe that he went there as a pilgrim, a voluntary exile for Christ, and to minister to the needs of those Dalriadic Irish who have settled in the western parts of Scotland, and to convert the Picts who have lived in those parts since ancient times. Just once or twice it is said that he returned to oversee the monasteries that he had founded at Durrow and at Kells, and because his exile was

58

too bitter for him. For sometimes he mourned for Derry from desolate Iona, for its leafy oak woods where white-winged angels dwell, and for his little cell among its groves.'

A moment of deep stillness fell upon them then. It was as if the fanning of a wing-tip, the breath of a holy presence, touched them both. Then Hilda quietly said,

'Iona is a place of great holiness.'

Aidan's gaunt face was radiant, 'It is an Island of the Blessed,' he said, 'though sometimes lashed by savage seas and gales, and often for days, weeks at a time, shrouded in mist and rain. But then the sun comes, and calm, and the turf shines like emerald, and the sea like sapphire and amethyst against the silver sand. And in every direction lie mystic islands and snow-clad peaks, and swallows skim the black peat bogs and the whispering rushes, and the air is filled with perfume from the flowers that lie like gems among the heather. And there is subsistence in plenty, fish, and wild berries and roots, sweet honey, and milk and cheese from the goats and sheep, and herbs and crops that the monks have planted. And in the evening when the sinking sun falls crimson on the billowing clouds that gather in the west, it is as if the angel host of Derry throngs there on pinions of gold and rose. Then the monks know the presence of God, and the dark and the cold and the heavy labour are not in vain.'

Again they were still, and then Aidan quietly turned to other matters. He questioned her closely about her studies, and was amazed at her learning, and when their young interpreter found the going too hard they conversed in Latin for Hilda now had a creditable grasp of the language. She knew that it was nearly time to go, for the tide would be creeping in again, but there was something that she hadn't said, and she looked at him shyly, hesitantly, and he looked back, understanding, waiting, for he knew what it would be.

'I hope one day to take vows,' she said, 'when I have studied more. But I do not wish to spend all my time then among cares that leave no space for contemplation and further study, and it seems that this can happen, even in the life of a nun. I believe that there are monasteries where more time is devoted to prayer and study. I know that there is one such at Chelles, in Gaul, for my sister Hereswith hopes to enter it as soon as she feels that the royal court of East Anglia no longer needs her, and there must be others like it.'

'It is something that we all must learn to discover,' he answered her gently. 'How contemplation can be practised within the life of action. It is not impossible. There are ways of withdrawing, of finding space within yourself, in the midst of pressing duties. You have great gifts of administration which perhaps should not be wasted. But I understand your need,' he said with compassion. 'The right course will become clear to you. There is plenty of time.'

'Oh yes,' she cried, imperious, confident again, 'I do not mean that it should be yet. Oswald will need me for some years, and I must study more. I am very content for the present. I just wanted you to know.'

'Thank you,' he said humbly. 'Thank you, my child, for seeking me out and telling me these things.'

She blushed that he should appear humble before her, and hung her head and regretted her tone, and thought of Columba who had been of royal blood, proud and obstinate, but who had learned humility.

'We shall often meet,' said Aidan, 'and I ask you to continue your work of love and service and conversion among the people, for you hold a unique position among them. You must think well about the vows that you would take. There can be no marriage, no children. There are royal alliances that you might make that could be of service to God.'

She thought fleetingly of Oswin but did not hesitate. 'That is something that I have no wish for. I have long been sure of that.' She answered him unflinchingly, as he had known that she would.

For eight years Oswald ruled Northumbria and united Deira and Bernicia again, for the people in both provinces loved him because of the life of simplicity and piety that he followed, while still remaining a powerful warrior who inspired the loyalty and courage among his thanes that kept Penda at bay and repelled his frequent incursions. He would refuse no plea from the poor and appointed a servant to be always at hand to relieve their needs.

'My Lord,' said this servant one Easter-time as the king sat down to dine with his bishop in celebration of the feast, 'there is a great crowd of needy folk sitting in the road outside begging alms from you.'

Oswald stood up and raised the great silver dish of succulent food from the table and handed it to his servants. 'Take it to them,' he ordered, 'and when they have eaten break up the dish itself and distribute the pieces among them.'

Aidan, greatly moved, clasped the generous right hand and blessed it, and asked of God that it might never perish.

The Irish monks, and the Anglo-Saxon novices under training at Lindisfarne, went among the people, teaching by example. And the people could see how Aidan, bishop of all Northumbria, ruled from his see at Lindisfarne but placed himself under the rule of its abbot and lived humbly, as a monk. At the same time James the deacon, and the monks of Paulinus who had remained, continued with their missionary work in Deira, and there seemed little conflict between the two traditions.

In these years Hilda moved between the townships and villages of the kingdom with boundless energy, seeing that the laws entitling the people to their rights were fairly carried out; that the butter and cheese makers, the dough-makers and cloth-workers among the women received their due, and the foresters and farm-workers their specified portions, and that the laws of inheritance and property were observed, so that she could inform the king of any injustice. She wanted nothing for herself and wore the simple garb of the people, and used her noble position and the wealth that she could command only in the service of the poor. And always in performing her tasks she struggled to achieve humility, and to curb her pride and quick temper. She continued with her studies, and although her tasks were secular she was always ready to teach and explain the scriptures to the unlettered people in their own tongue, for she had a good command of Latin and could study the gospels which were being copied by the monks so that more might circulate among those who could read them.

And at this time the boy Cuthbert learns through a miracle that it is time for him to lay aside the carefree pleasures of childhood and to follow another calling.

And the noble youth Wilfrid, raised in the ways of the court by his father, will soon set out, sumptuously caparisoned and escorted as befits his birth, for the royal palace. There he will seek the patronage of the queen to gain entry to the monastery of Lindisfarne, so that he may begin his search for the kingdom of Heaven.

And above the marshy estuary of the Esk river, on the grassy cliff that towers above the settlement of Streanshalch that one day the Danes will call Whitby, the herdsman Caedmon, who comes of British stock, tends the animals in his charge. He watches the ebb and flow of the tides, and the movement of the sun and moon and the wandering stars. He knows the rhythm of the seasons, and he sees that in all things there is a pattern. A wonder fills him that he longs to pour out in song. Only there is no music. There are no words.

PART II

The Remainder of Her Life

CHAPTER 6

On the fifth day of August, in the year AD 642, Oswald was slain in battle by Penda at Maserfield, that would later be called Oswestry. He died calling upon God to preserve the souls of his men, as the enemy closed in upon him. His followers severed his right hand and arm and placed them in a silver casket that was taken to the church of St Peter in the royal township of Bamburgh. There they remained uncorrupted, as Aidan had fortold. And many miracles were reported at the place on the field of battle where Oswald fell. He was followed as King by his younger brother Oswy, and not by his own son Ethelwald as he had intended. Oswy was waiting his opportunity and acted swiftly to seize the succession, and at first shared the kingdom with Oswin, prince of Deira, as Oswald had done. But conflict and mistrust grew between the two for Oswy was ambitious for wealth and power, and Northumbria became divided again, and the people mourned for the saintly king Oswald.

Hilda strove to be loyal to Oswy, but she could not hold him in the loving respect that had bound her to Oswald and to Edwin before him, and she was filled with restlessness and a sudden weariness of her ceaseless activity. She was now twenty-eight years old and her longing to follow the monastic way of life, and to leave the land and the people that she loved as an exile for Christ, became overwhelming. And it was at about this time that messengers came from her sister Hereswith to say that she would now enter the monastery at Chelles, for her husband had died in battle against Penda and her sons had grown to manhood. But the times were very troubled again in Northumbria and Hilda bowed

65

obediently to Aidan's advice that the people still needed her. Then news came to her that Oswy would take as his second wife Enfleda, the daughter of Edwin and Ethelburga, the child who Hilda had dearly loved and parted from when she was six years old and fled with her mother and Paulinus to Kent after Edwin was killed. Hilda's spirits rose again and she knew that her right course was to stay as she was, and to help the young queen to assume her duties in the Northumbrian court just as she had once done for Ethelburga.

Oswy's bride made the journey by sea, and was only saved from death in a violent storm because Aidan had thought to provide the priest who was sent to fetch her with a holy oil that had power to calm the raging waters.

It was joy to Hilda to be re-united with the girl, who was at this time about twenty years old and had never forgotten her mother's loved companion. She brought greetings to Hilda from Ethelburga, abbess now of the nunnery at Lyming that she had founded. She told her that Paulinus had lately died, after many years as bishop of Rochester.

'And the little ones, Wuscfrea and Iffi who escaped with you?' Hilda asked gently, fearing the answer.

Enfleda looked away, 'They were sent to France,' she said, 'they died there soon afterwards, still in infancy.'

The new queen was glad to find that there were still priests in Northumbria who had been ordained by Paulinus, and that although Oswy observed the law and liturgy of the Ionan tradition he saw no reason for her to change from the practices in which she was brought up. He was indeed most fully aware of the advantages of renewing the alliance with Kent, and soon allowed her to send there for Romanus, who was her own chaplain. Enfleda loved and admired Hilda but could not understand how her devotion to Aidan and the Irish ways could have come about, when she had been first instructed and baptised by Paulinus.

For five more years Hilda dutifully served the king and his people, and then her restlessness became too great to bear. The stomach pains that she had long ago recovered from returned to trouble her, and at night she tossed and turned upon her pallet and could find no rest. A resolve came over her. She must go away somewhere to be alone and to think. She would journey to East Anglia to the court of her nephew Aldwulf, Hereswith's son, and stay there for a time under his protection. Then, if it seemed God's will, she would follow her sister to Chelles. She would not consult Aidan for he might again dissuade her, and this time she knew that she was right. She had fulfilled her tasks. She was of royal blood and free at last to do as she felt called. Quietly and quickly she made her preparations, telling only those closest to her what she would do and asking that no-one should try to dissuade or follow her. In the spring of the year AD 647 she set out with a small company of loyal attendants and left Northumbria.

The long journey to the royal palace of East Anglia, where Hilda had spent her infancy, was made with good speed. The party was small and fast moving, and attracted no attention. Hilda had chosen attendants who were as hardy as herself, ready to travel from dawn each day until the short summer nightfall. Aldwulf, king now of the East Angles, welcomed his kinswoman warmly and with sympathy for her request to live in retirement at his court. There were other like-minded women among the royal family, women who would take the veil and in the course of time found monasteries. And there was opportunity for study and for meeting with scholars. The monastery founded by the Irish monk Fursey was well established as a seat of learning, and the Burgundian bishop of the East Angles, Felix, had founded a school in his see of Dunwich where monks from Canterbury taught on the Gaulish model. Hilda could see no conflict there between the two traditions.

67

She spent long hours in study, and in prayer and meditation, yet the peace that she was seeking did not come and often she was restless and asked if she could undertake small tasks among the sick and poor, but always taking care that she did not usurp an authority that was not hers. Often she regretted that she had not spoken to Aidan and would have sent him messages, only no-one was travelling to Northumbria because winter was setting in.

Nearly a year passed and still Hilda could not tell her right course; she who had been so unhesitating, always so sure of what was right. Pain still troubled her and she could not eat. Spring returned, and with it fair winds, and the trading vessels began their journeys again from the Deben and the Ouse. She watched them setting out from the river mouths for Gaul, and a longing filled her and she determined that at last she would take such a vessel, find her sister whom she pined to see again, seek peace in the veil and become a nun in the monastery at Chelles. The king agreed readily to her request. A ship was found that would take her when it was ready, and her servants began to prepare for the journey.

It was then that the messengers came from Aidan. Two young monks stood before Hilda, worn from their journey because word of her imminent departure had reached them as they neared the royal palace and they had travelled day and night.

'We have come from Aidan,' said the older of the two. 'The king has given him a hide of land on the north bank of the river Wear for the establishment of a small monastery. Aidan wishes to grant this to you, that you may begin to observe the monastic rule there with a handful of companions of your own choice.'

Pain clutched her stomach and the blood drained from her cheeks, but she drew herself up.

'It is a command?' she said.

The young priest looked her steadily in the eye, so that she should not see how much he was alarmed by the fierce, gaunt face above him.

'Aidan asks your obedience,' he answered quietly.

She flushed and looked away, then looking back imperiously replied, 'I do not have to return at Aidan's bidding. My mind is made up that I go to Chelles, for I believe it to be God's will that I do so and I have given the matter earnest prayer.'

She paused and looked at them both and saw with sudden compassion how tired they were, and how young, and frightened of her, and she summoned a servant to see that they were well fed and comfortably accommodated.

She smiled at them, 'You shall have my answer tomorrow,' she said, and already she knew what it must be.

'I will return with you to Northumbria,' she told them the next day, looking into their faces with calm and clear grey eyes, 'As Aidan has requested. But you shall rest here for a few days first and meet the scholars trained by Fursey and by Felix. And I must prepare myself and my companions and ask Aldwulf for an escort perhaps, through the most dangerous parts.'

'Oswy has sent a strong escort for you,' the young monk replied. 'They were a few days behind us on the road, and should soon be here.'

Hilda smiled wryly, 'So he knew that I would return' she said. The young man smiled back. He did not any longer fear her.

'Aidan said that you would,' he answered.

So Hilda went back to Northumbria and her escort followed in reverse the route that Lilla had chosen so many years before when he took her as an infant with her mother to Edwin's protection at Redwald's court; crossing the fens westward to Peterborough: travelling the raised causeway of the Romans to Lincoln, where Bregusyth had encountered Botulf: fording the rivers Calder, Don and Idle: and searching out the tracks in the dry patches of the Humber marshlands to reach the great forested plain of York. Here the party struck eastward towards the coast, skirting for safety the high, remote ridges that lay beyond the plain and were the haunt of robbers and wild beasts. The coastal track climbed round the high cliffs of Deira and through its fishing villages, and one golden day of late summer the travellers came to the great cliff at Whitby where the blue North Sea rollers broke white against the black cliffs, and the crimson heather spread west to the horizon. And Caedmon the herdsman, tending his goats upon the cliff, watched them pass by. Then they came inland again to avoid the marshy estuaries of the rivers Esk and Tees, and so to the high moorlands of Bernicia and the Roman wall whose parallel causeway they followed back to the coast; until at last they saw against the skyline the royal township of Bamburgh and the waves thundering against the rock beneath its fortress, for by this time the gales of autumn were blowing.

The long journey held no hardship for Hilda. Her spirit was lightening, lifting as if a burden had fallen from her shoulders. She rejoiced in the movement and the adventure. She watched the seasons move from spring to autumn, saw the budding of the womb-warm earth, and the young born upon it, and the miraculous blooming. Her heart sang within her. Her appetite and vigour returned. It was a time for meditation on the passages of scripture that she knew now by heart, and on all that she had learned and for reflection on the pattern that her life was taking. She began to think about the rule that she would make for her small community, and who she would choose as her first nuns.

As soon as she could she went to visit Aidan, and her eyes filled with tears when she saw him, and she could hardly speak.

'You knew that I would come,' she said. 'Forgive me for going as I did.' She hesitated. 'I was so sure that I was right.'

'You were right,' he answered gently. 'It was the only way to discover your true vocation. Do you begin to see how the threads of your calling weave together again, although they have spread in another pattern for a time? That pattern becomes a part of the whole design, and makes it more intricate and of greater worth. Nothing has been wasted. But it has been hard for you.'

'Yes,' she replied ruefully, 'when my father named me Hilda, meaning Conflict, he did not know how right he was.

70

He was thinking of battles of a different nature.' She looked at him mischievously, 'And what if I had gone to Chelles?' she asked.

'It would have been further for my monks to travel,' he said, his eyes twinkling, 'And an even longer return journey for you.'

She looked at him humbly, 'I do not deserve that you should need me so much,' she said. 'You must tell me what you want me to do.'

'We will make plans immediately,' he answered. 'But first I too have forgiveness to ask.' She looked at him in surprise, and saw laughter still in his eyes:

'That an Irish priest of the people should send such peremptory orders to a daughter of Woden,' he said. She laughed and flushed in confusion, but saw that there was kindness still in his face.

'It is a small plot only, that the king has granted,' Aidan went on seriously, 'it will not support many people. Oswy thinks that Oswald has endowed monasteries enough. But the people who live in the villages beside the river Wear are poor, and Christianity means little to them yet. They are in need of a community who will care for them and love them, as well as teach them. There you will take your vows and be clothed as a nun, with the other women you will choose. Priests will visit you to administer the sacraments, and I will come myself sometimes. But your rule you will make as you think fit, within the framework of the Church. It is a beginning for you. You will know of the abbess Heiu who founded the monastery at Hartlepool and was the first woman in Northumbria to take the veil with my blessing. She begins to find the task too great, because the monastery is growing very fast, and besides her heart is in Deira among her own people and her loyalty is to Oswin, and not to Oswy who she does not trust. You will know that there is bitter rivalry again between the two kingdoms. I know that soon Heiu will ask to be relieved in order to return to her kin. When she feels ready to do so I would like you to take her place.'

Hilda bowed her head in obedience. 'You feel that women

have an important part to play in the Church?' she asked him.

'An essential one,' he answered, 'and one instigated by Jesus himself. Has it struck you, as you study the scriptures, how different was his attitude to women from that of Jewish tradition, which expected them to be subservient, silent and segregated, and not thought worthy of religious instruction? It must have been hard for those first Jewish Christians to accept so radical a change, just as it was hard for them to understand that Jesus had come to redeem the whole Gentile world and not just their own race. You will remember how Jesus encouraged Mary to listen to his teaching instead of helping Martha with the household tasks, and how women were always among his closest friends and followers: how they never deserted him and were first at the tomb on Easter morning: how Jesus made his first appearance as risen Lord to Mary Magdalene and entrusted her with reporting it, at a time when the evidence of women would have been discounted. In the early days the church was greatly dependent on them, for teaching and evangelising as well as for hosting its meetings in their homes. To this St Paul testifies, although as a traditional Jew he had difficulty there, and also a great fear of the distraction of women, for carnal reasons.'

Hilda smiled, 'I have noticed that. But he also gave them their due, and in the Epistle to the Galatians teaches that in union with Jesus Christ all are made one, that there is no such thing as Jew and Greek, slave and freeman, male and female.'

'That is a significant passage,' the bishop agreed. 'What matters is that the Word was made Flesh. At the time and place that God chose for his Incarnation only a man could have done the things that He had to do. But I have observed, since I came to work amongst the Anglo-Saxon people, in what high regard the women of your race are held. Their rights are carefully protected, and they are the guardians of wisdom and learning. Their warrior lords defer to them in all such matters.'

'That is true,' said Hilda, 'but more in the case of the

nobly born. It is partly why I long to bring learning and understanding to all the people, high and low alike.'

'You must make every opportunity to do so.' Aidan looked at her in affectionate accord, and an enduring trust and friendship was born between them.

Soon Hilda was clothed as a nun, and knew beyond all doubt that this was her vocation.

It was no hardship for her to exchange the garments of her secular life for the habit of rough unbleached woollen cloth, and the linen wimple that must hide her cropped brown hair. Ever since she was a child she had shunned the rich apparel and fine jewels of the court that would have set her apart from the people she served. Now she gladly brought her few personal possesions to be held in common by the community.

Then she was blessed by Aidan and made her vows: of poverty, that she had already embraced: of chastity, without which she could never give her whole being to her work: of obedience to God's will and to her superiors and to the rule that she herself would make. The last was for her the hardest of the three vows because it meant patience, and the humbling of her pride, and the submission of her own strong will.

From among the women closest to her she chose a small number who were ready and willing to share her religious life. Some like herself were of noble birth and already learned in the scriptures, others were lowly-born and ignorant, but very sure of their vocation. Hilda allowed no difference to be made between them. All of them were ready to make their full vows. There was as yet no provision for the training of novices. In addition she appointed lay sisters, women from the villages who were ready to serve among the nuns but who did not make vows.

The needs of the small nunnery were very simple and could be supplied by the local people, who were glad of the trade that it brought them and ready to labour with the nuns in cultivating their plot of land. The lay sisters brought in the sick and the poor, for the nuns must remain within the enclosure of the monastery once they had taken their vows, and the Gospel began to spread among the villages beside the Wear.

But very soon Aidan came to tell Hilda that the abbess Heiu wished now to leave the monastery at Hartlepool and return to her kinsfolk in the Deiran town of Tadcaster, as he had known that she would.

'Is it too soon to ask you to leave your nunnery and become abbess of Hartlepool?' he asked her, for he could see how happy she was.

'I am ready.' Unhesitatingly she answered. 'Things will run smoothly here now without me, for everyone works together for the common good. They will scarcely notice that I have gone!'

Aidan shook his head. 'You will be sadly missed. The people love you. I have heard the youngest of the novices and the humblest of the people call you Mother.'

'It gives me such joy when they do,' Hilda said. 'I strive to be as one of them. I know that sometimes I frighten them without intending it — when they are slow to obey or understand.'

'It is hard always to be patient,' he said, 'and a little firm authority does no harm. But Hartlepool you will find very different. It has grown fast, for the land can support a large community. You will have monks as well as nuns under your charge as you know, and young novices, and lay people too, and the ordering of the liturgy and of your rule, and the direction of study.'

'I am ready,' she repeated eagerly, 'to undertake all these matters. I will take with me the two nuns Frigyth and Edith for I shall delegate some of the administration to them, and also Begu for she needs my care still. I have trained others ready to replace them.'

It was clear to Aidan that she was not only ready, but prepared.

The double monastery of Hartlepool was built upon the rocky cliff that juts beyond the swamps of the broad Tees estuary. Westward from its ramparts some of the dense woodland had been cleared and cultivated, and people from the nearby settlements worked alongside the inmates, farming the land, weaving, brewing and baking. On the plan that Hilda had already seen at Coldingham the monks and nuns lived in segregated quarters built of thatch and timber, but they joined together for study, and for worship in the church that stood at the centre of the settlement. Near it was a library where texts of the scriptures and the fathers were studied and copied, and an infirmary where the sick and poor came in great numbers. Closer to the ramparts lay the workshops, and beyond them the farm buildings. It was a thriving and self-sufficient community.

Hilda held all these threads in her hands. But besides the two nuns Frigyth and Edith she soon found others among the inmates at Hartlepool ready to work under her in positions of trust, the more so when they saw how little she spared herself. And the nun Begu, so slow in learning, but so sure of her vocation, was ready to undertake the humblest of tasks if only she might serve the abbess.

Hilda's chief concern was for the care of the sick and needy, for the training of the novices, and for the encouragement of scholarship. The harbours and rivermouths of the north-east provided easy access to the south of the country and to the continent, and there was a constant coming and going of scholars, a generous loaning of books and a ready interchange of ideas that brought an energy and a blossoming into the Northumbrian monasteries, so near to one another yet each so diverse and original.

There was at that time no single universally prescribed

rule of monastic life, and there were several that Hilda could study and adapt to the needs of her community of Hartlepool. She did not care for those rules that she thought over-harsh and too much concerned with subduing the flesh. Those under her charge led exacting enough lives already. She was moved by the stories that were recounted of Columba, who would not allow fasting and privation beyond endurance. It was told how he had admonished the Abbot of Durrow for forcing his monks outside for heavy labour in the cruellest winter weather. She had learned of those instructions sent by Pope Gregory the Great, that wisest of counsellors, to Augustine of Canterbury for the care of his flock, that allowed for such flexibility and such compassion for what mankind must bear. She saw that the spirit of the law must always be greater than the letter, and justice tempered with mercy. She strove for a monastic way that was orderly and workable; time for prayer and time for study; time for labour and for rest; and always, in all things, the observance of every virtue, especially charity and peace. She would have no one rich or poor, for so it had been in the primitive church. Everything was held in common and no one possessed personal property.

Aidan was growing frail. He spent less time now in missionary work and was often in the remote hermitage that he loved on the Farne Island, or in the simple lodgings that the queen kept always ready for him at the royal residences. She loved the bishop for his Christlike life and goodness, though her chaplain Romanus, who had come with her from Kent, insisted that he was mistaken in his customs. Aidan still visited Hilda when he could, and they spent many hours together in discussion, and she felt a humble wonder at his need of her now, and that he went away from her refreshed.

There were many who came to the abbess for advice, the king and queen among them. Enfleda loved her, and Oswy knew that he could trust her as he could few others. Always he lived under the threat from Penda, and there were open conflicts and rivalries within his own kingdom too. Oswald's son, Ethelwald, was waiting his opportunity to seize power, and Oswy could not rule peacably with Oswin as Oswald had done. He wished to reign supreme in Northumbria and to hold Deira ready for his own son, Alchfrid, born of an earlier marriage and coming now to manhood. It was bitter to Hilda that Christian kings should be so warlike. She had seen how they could live in peace. Yet she knew too how deeply ingrained in the people of her race was the pride of battle and the worship of their heroic kings. Even the pious Oswin, the gentle handsome giant so loved by everyone, was a mighty warrior ready to fight for his kingdom if Oswy would not live at peace with him.

It is the summer of the year AD 651. Oswy raises his forces to march against Oswin, and Oswin summons his own army. Then Oswin discovers that the forces against him far outnumber his own, that defeat is certain. He must wait for a more favourable opportunity and not risk the slaughter of his men.

He disbands them at a place called Wilfar's Hill that lies north west of Catterick, and sends them home. He finds refuge for himself and a companion at the house of his dearest and most trusted friend, a nobleman called Hunwald. But Hunwald is no friend. He knows that Oswin's betrayal will bring great rewards; lands and riches, power and the friendship of the king. And Oswy does not hesitate. As soon as he learns from Hunwald of Oswin's hiding place he sends his commander to murder him.

There is universal horror and disgust at such a crime. Hilda bows in bitter sorrow for the ways of men. The queen is torn with anguish that her lord can do such a thing. The bishop Aidan, sick now in his last illness, is staying in a shelter made for him against the west wall of the little church at Oswy's country house near Bamburgh. He has but lately dined with Oswin, and knows him doomed. When the news is broken to him Aidan leans his head in sorrow against an upright of the church, and dies.

The same night the shepherd lad Cuthbert, watching over his master's flocks in the Lammermuir hills, receives a vision of the heavenly host streaming earthwards through the darkness to take up the soul of the bishop. He knows it as a sign that he himself is ready now to take up the religious life.

The monks of Lindisfarne bear Aidan's body across the causeway and bury it in the cemetery of the monks, as he would have wished. In later years, when a great stone church will be built, his bones shall have more fitting burial beside its altar.

Then the people of Deira turned to Ethelwald, son of Oswald, to rule them in place of Oswin, and Ethelwald, fearing Oswy, placed himself under Penda's protection, so that Deira was brought under the sway of the powerful pagan king.

Enfleda saw how bitter and angry the people had been made by her husband's treachery, and that something must be done at once in expiation, to show that he repented. She petitioned him for land at the place of Oswin's murder, at Ingetlingum, that would be called Gilling, which is not far from Richmond. Here a monastery was built by the monk Trumhere, chosen because he was of Anglo-Saxon birth and close relative of the king, but trained and ordained in the Ionan tradition. Here would be offered prayer for the salvation of both Oswin and Oswy, for slain and slayer together.

The queen was growing anxious too at the tension that she could see was mounting between the king and his son Alchfrid, ambitious now for power and beginning to look for issues of conflict with his father. Heavily influenced by Romanus in favour of the traditions of Canterbury, Alchfrid scorned Oswy's adherence to Ionan ways and followed the customs used by his stepmother.

The times were dark, and the people not yet appeased for Oswin's murder. They went in fear of Penda's constant attacks, and his continued threat to the kingdoms of Northumbria whose position was weakened by Oswy's act of treachery. The power of Mercia was growing fast. Thanks to Penda's firm alliance with the British king of Gwynedd on his western border, and a recent treaty with the king of the East Anglians, he was free to concentrate all his forces on the Northumbrian front. Oswy had to act. He was no coward, but he knew the might of Penda's army; thirty times greater than his own it was said; thirty battle-hardened legions under famous commanders. Desperately he offered Penda all the wealth at his command; his royal regalia, gold and precious stones and other gifts, as the price of peace and as ransom for another of his sons held hostage at the court of Mercia. But the king of Mercia, seeing Northumbria in his grasp, refused every offer. Oswy must go to war, whatever the odds.

The king was well aware that God could be enlisted as a political ally, that he might be persuaded to aid a Christian king in grave straits as he had Oswald at Heavenfield, or be open to a bargain such as Edwin had made when he offered the infant Enfleda for baptism, and then his own conversion, in return for victory. An infant daughter! A fair offer occurred to Oswy. It was the year AD 655 and the little daughter born him by the queen was one year old. He vowed that if God would grant him victory then the child Elfleda would be dedicated to His service, in perpetual virginity. And he would bequeath to the church the land and wealth that were her right of inheritance, enough for the founding of twelve mon- asteries, six in Deira and six in Bernicia. Surely God would be agreeable to such a bargain, and the people placated too. Enfleda agreed to the arrangement with equanimity, for she was determined that in the event the child should go to Hilda at Hartlepool. She knew the joy that this care would bring to the abbess. She herself would see her daughter often, and besides, she would bear other children.

In the autumn of that year word reached Oswy that Penda's army was approaching Deira from the south west. It was reinforced by the armies of Wales, and by those promised by the East Anglian king. With such superior might the pagan warlord was confident that at last he could carry out his boasted intention to wipe out Oswy's people, from the highest to the lowest in the kingdom. It was reported that Ethelwald had guided the armies into the Humber marshlands, made yet more treacherous by heavy rain, and left them in position there. He would take no further part in the battle against his own kin, and withdrew to await the outcome in a place of safety.

Oswy and Alchfrid summoned their warriors and marched against Penda. They took up their position along the low, rain-sodden banks of the river Winwaed, close to where it joined the Don and wound through swamplands to the Humber estuary. The land was drear and waterlogged, and when the opposing armies joined in battle the rain began to fall again in torrents. Then the swollen Winwaed burst its banks and flooded the surrounding country.

Oswy's forces, who knew better where the ridges of firm land would lie below the swirling water, at once seized their advantage. They flung themselves upon the floundering enemy, forcing them out of their depths. The flooding river claimed more victims than the sword. The armies of Mercia were destroyed. Penda died with his invincible commanders, and with those treacherous princes who had betrayed their kinsmen and their former allies.

As soon as the campaign was ended, and a peace concluded in the region of Loidis, that would be called Leeds, Oswy lost no time in sending among the Mercians those Anglo-Saxon missionaries trained by Aidan at Lindisfarne, to preach to them in their own tongue and convert them to Christianity. He also arranged for one of these missionaries, the priest Cedd, to be consecrated as bishop to the East Saxons, whose ruler Oswy had himself persuaded to receive baptism. And at about this time he agreed to the marriage of his daughter Alchfleda to Peada, son of Penda and ruler under his father of the kingdom of the middle Angles, on condition that he became a Christian.

The people could see that without any doubt Oswy had gone far towards redeeming his crime against Oswin, and was doing all that he could to show his gratitude to God for so mighty a victory.

Then the child Elfleda was dedicated to God and given to the abbess Hilda in the monastery at Hartlepool. And Hilda was overwhelmed with joy that God had granted her this blessing and took the baby into her keeping as if it were her own. The nun Begu tended to all the little one's needs, but the child was never far from Hilda, and knew her as mother.

CHAPTER 7

ilda has come now to the time of her life work; to the founding of the monastery at Whitby that will carry her name down the centuries. Here the pattern of her life will become part of the great design of the growing church. For it is the wish both of Finan, bishop of Lindisfarne in succession to Aidan, and of Oswy, High King now after Penda's defeat and a powerful influence throughout the land, that Hilda shall found the greatest of the twelve monasteries on the lands that are Elfleda's portion, and choose for herself the site that she will have.

Christianity was well established in Bernicia, thanks to Aidan's tireless missionaries, and it seemed to the abbess that the church in Deira had the greater need because the people's faith was still shaken by the treachery of their Christian rulers, and the monks of Lindisfarne had made less headway there.

'You will choose your site in Deira?' the queen asked her anxiously. She had come to Hartlepool to see Elfleda, as she sometimes did, for parting with the child had been harder than she expected, and the little girl sat upon her knees playing with a golden bracelet sent by her father. Enfleda was quick to see the diplomatic advantage that would lie in an abbess who was kin to Oswy, and Hilda saw it too, though not as a reason for her choice. But she loved Enfleda and understood the conflicts that she faced in her loyalty to the king, and to her ambitious stepson Alcfrith.

'I will choose a site in Deira,' she said gently. 'There are many reasons why it would be best — most importantly the need among the people there. Aidan's monks have been more in Bernicia, and Deira has been left to the monks of Kent and so conversion has lagged behind.' She looked at her young kinswoman quizzically and Enfleda raised an eyebrow. Their differences did not alter their affection for each other and were resolved in banter.

'It is not so,' Enfleda replied firmly, 'conversion in Deira goes well. James the deacon has a great following in York and Catterick, although he grows old now and less concerned with missionary work. And you will know that Alcfrith has given estates for a new monastery at Ripon and that abbott Eata has moved there from Melrose with his monks. They are of the Irish persuasion, trained at Lindisfarne, but Alcfrith believes that they will change their customs. Then I have enabled the young monk Wilfrid to journey from Lindisfarne to Rome. He shows rare promise and wishes to study there, and Finan has let him go willingly, and he is accompanied by the monk Benedict Biscop who shares Wilfrid's ambitions. I have the highest hopes of what these two will accomplish for the Church when they return. But what site would you choose in Deira?'

Hilda's face shone. The choice was easy. She had never forgotten riding through the heather to come upon the towering cliff of Whitby on that golden day of autumn as she returned from East Anglia to take her vows.

'Whitby is one of the sites that Oswy would give,' she answered. 'It is a holy place and I think that God calls me there. It is lonely, sea-girt, beautiful, yet not so remote that scholars may not reach it both by sea and by land. The valley of the Esk river is fertile, once clearances are made in the woodland, and the moorland will support some livestock and may be tilled where it borders the valley.'

So the abbess rode to Whitby to look again at the lands there. The cold waves of the North Sea drove up the wide estuary of the Esk, and at the foot of the west cliff was a broad marshy area that made that part difficult of access, but the high east cliff was dry and rocky and could be reached from the crossing place at Spital Bridge, higher up the river where the Spital Beck joined its waters. Here a track ran beside the river to the village of Whitby, whose inhabitants lived by fishing and trading and by husbanding their clearances in the forests of the Esk valley.

Twilight is falling as Hilda climbs the steep track to the summit of the cliff. Under her feet lie the tumbled stones of a Roman signal station built by men who brought into Britain strange cults and an alien pantheon. Among them came those first Christians, unnamed, unrecorded, so close in time to Jesus Christ that they might have spoken to him, seen him, touched him, or known those who did. She looks out across the darkening sea, sailed by her pirate ancestors who brought with them legends of the Northern gods from the cold shores beyond. Forerunners of the one God, these ancient deities; men groping for the Truth that will be made known to them when the time is ripe for their race to be brought into the pattern of Christianity.

Caedmon watches from his hut further down the cliff and sees the tall figure outlined against the sky, between the earth and the pricking stars. He thinks it some goddess from those songs that stir his soul when the harp is passed round and he sits in his accustomed corner beyond the firelight and will not take his turn, because the force within him cannot be unlocked. Hilda turns and comes back down the path, picking her way carefully for it is dark now, to the village below, where she has lodging for the night. Caedmon stands by the path to see her more closely and she pauses to speak to him, but seeing that there is fear in his eyes she does not try to detain him when he turns quickly away towards his hut. But she has glimpsed something in the haunted face that startles and arrests her.

She rode back to Hartlepool next day, sure that she had found the place for her monastery. The blood coursed through her veins like wine and she began to make her plans; how her rule would remain as she had devised it at Hartlepool, and her first care always the needs of her people; how some of her scholars would accompany her and help her to found at Whitby a school of great learning; how she would collect a fine library and have the sacred texts copied by the most skilled of scribes and illuminators. Word of her intentions must go out at once. There would be music in her church — her old friend James would send monks from York to train the choir. Stone crosses would stand in the monastery precinct, carved with the Gospel stories and with symbols of the faith that would reach into the understanding of the unlettered. The segregated monks and nuns would have individual small cells, so that they could pray and study in solitude. These should be grouped near the central place where the principle church, dedicated to St Peter, would be constructed. A house for novices would be built nearer to the boundary of the monastery, and in this area too would be the larger buildings for general use, dwellings for lay inmates and visitors, and those of the craftsmen and labourers. At Whitby Elfleda would grow up, and one day succeed herself as abbess.

But first there were practical matters. Land must be cleared and wells and drainage dug, and timber seasoned so that the first buildings could be erected. A workforce must be found ready to undertake the heavy labour of building and cultivation for fair reward, because the monasteries refused to employ slaves and indeed it was the policy of the church, following Aidan's example, to purchase their freedom whenever this could be done.

By the year AD 657, preparation enough had been made for Hilda to move to Whitby with the twelve monks and twelve nuns chosen to accompany her from Hartlepool. Among them was the monk Oftor, who in time would be made bishop of Worcester, and the nun Frigyth to be in charge of novices, and Begu to care for Elfleda.

The child Elfleda grew sturdy and vigorous, and because there were other children in the monastery, boys and girls promised like herself to the church, she did not lack playmates. Imperious and strong-willed, she was from an early age conscious of her royal blood, for the king and queen on their occasional visits did not allow her to forget it. Oswy indeed regretted his promise a little when he saw that she would grow beautiful, and might have made him a powerful alliance. She was made much of by those ladies of noble family who had taken refuge in the monastery. They indulged her pleasure in adorning herself by giving her the gems and trinkets that she loved. Yet she was generous and open-hearted too, and shared her treasures with her companions, and she was loving and obedient to Hilda, who reared her with tolerance. Her childhood would be short enough and all too soon she must renounce such things.

Sometimes the children would find their way to the farm buildings and watch how the herdsman Caedmon cared for the animals so tenderly; the newborn whose parents would not suckle them, and the sick and injured. He welcomed the children and was at ease with them. They could not understand one another's speech for he spoke in the tongue of the Britons, but there was no need for words between them.

'He let me hold a tiny kid,' Elfleda told Hilda excitedly one spring day when she was about seven years old, 'but it kicked and wriggled. It would not lie still in my arms as it does in his. And do you know, Mother, that he sleeps among the animals? And outside his hut there are flowers growing. He has taken seeds and little plants from the cliffs and the woods so that he can watch them grow and blossom. You ought to go and see!'

Hilda did not answer at once. Then she said hesitantly, 'I would like to go and see, but he is always frightened of me, I do not know why. He turns away if I try to speak to him.'

'Well you are rather frightening,' said Elfleda. 'You don't mean to be,' she added reassuringly. 'You don't frighten me, or Begu. But you do look rather like an eagle, and you are so very tall and Caedmon is not.'

Hilda laughed. She loved the child's directness and knew that she meant no disrespect. Then she sighed, for she could not help her height, her aquiline face, now gaunt, her deepset piercing grey eyes, her commanding presence.

'I would like to make friends with Caedmon,' she said.

'You can't,' said Elfleda wisely. 'He's frightened of others too. Begu has talked to some of the people and they say that he will never take his turn in the storytelling when the mead flows and the harp is passed round. And they know that he could, for he talks to the animals, and even to the plants, and tells them stories as if they were human. And sometimes he holds stones in his hands, smooth pebbles from the beach, and pieces of wood, and touches them so gently with his fingers, as if he feared that he might hurt them; as if they were alive.'

Hilda mused for a while after the child had gone to find Begu. She too had seen how Caedmon did these things, as if he held all matter to be sacred. And she had seen him stand in wonder before the sculptured stonework of the crosses, tracing the carving with his fingers, or sometimes with his ear pressed against the church wall while the choir was practising. She must wait with patience. God would show her a way of reaching him.

At about this time Wilfrid returned to Northumbria. A monk now, tonsured in the manner of Rome, after three years spent studying in Gaul and Italy. He was passionately convinced of the authenticity of the Roman tradition and determined that it must be established throughout the Church, and he was profoundly influenced by the example set by the bishops he had encountered on the continent. They were aristocrats who took their place among the greatest in the land. They had acquired considerable estates and great wealth, and the patronage, power and prestige that went with it. They dedicated this power to pastoral purposes, founding monasteries, caring for the sick and poor, teaching the young and having authority to correct and direct both kings and rulers. They combined public lives of pomp and munificence with private ones of holiness and austerity in a manner that appealed mightily to Wilfrid but was a far cry from the ways of Aidan and of Columba.

Back again at Oswy's court, Wilfrid saw an opportunity in friendship with the king's son Alcfrith, sub-king of Deira, and already a strong advocate for the ways of Rome. The two young men were of an age and became close companions. Alcfrith was flattered that Wilfrid should seek him out, for he was dazzled by the breadth of his friend's grasp of matters theological and ecclesiastical and by his remarkable eloquence, and won by his undoubted charm and his enjoyment of pomp and circumstance and every courtly pursuit. He began to regret that he had appointed Eata to the monastery and rich lands of Ripon. Eata had been one of the twelve Anglo-Saxon boys taken for training by Aidan when he first founded Lindisfarne, and he held fast to the ways that he had learned there and would not change as Alcfrith had expected. Alcfrith took this continuing reluctance as an opportunity to oust him and to give the monastery of Ripon to his favourite. Eata, faced with an ultimatum, agreed to return to Melrose and most of his monks chose to accompany him, among them the young Cuthbert, who had been guestmaster of Ripon. The people were grieved to see the monks go, for they loved and respected them. Cuthbert especially drew crowds wherever he went, and travelled far afield to preach and convert in remote and dangerous parts where ordinary folk feared to go. It was said that he made no provision for himself but was miraculously fed and sheltered wherever he went. It was in the year AD 660 that Eata went back to Melrose, and in the following year Cuthbert was made prior there.

So Wilfrid was appointed to Ripon and arrived there in state with his entourage, and with gangs of carpenters and masons to replace the simple hutments and small wooden church of his predecessors so that the treasures he had brought from Rome, pictures and precious vessels, relics and altar hangings, could be properly housed, and himself and his court fittingly accommodated. The people watched in amazement as the foundations of stone buildings were laid on a new site, and craftsmen skilled in stone, glass and metal work made their way to Ripon from the south. And they wondered at the wealth and lifestyle of the new abbot, who kept his own clerks and retainers, his armed guard and his huntsmen and fowlers, like any nobleman.

But for some time Wilfrid remained a deacon, refusing ordination by Colman, bishop of Lindisfarne in succession to Finan, because he feared that priesthood from such hands might not be valid. It was not until the French priest Agilbert, bishop of the West Saxons, could perform the ceremony, during a visit to Alcfrith in York, that Wilfrid received the laying on of hands that made him a priest and therefore eligible for episcopal office.

Now the dispute between the Roman and Celtic churches was becoming more open, and the many points of ecclesiastical order upon which they differed were being studied by a new generation of scholars in the Northumbrian church who were in closer contact with Canterbury, and less sensitive to the charisma of Aidan and to the memory of Columba and the founders of Irish monasticism. First among these scholars was a priest named Ronan, himself an Irishman, who had studied in Gaul and Italy. The force of his arguments in favour of Rome convinced many of the Northumbrian clergy and raised doubts in their minds about the validity of Holy Orders, and therefore of the sacraments, in the monastic systems. Because episcopal consecration was not according to the canonical rites of the Roman church, they began to fear that the people might not be receiving the true faith. There was a feeling that the veneration in which Aidan had been held by high and low alike, even by churchmen of the Roman persuasion in the south, had allowed these differences to continue for too long.

Yet the issues could not be distinguished clearly between the usages of the Celtic church and those established as a result of Augustine's mission in the south, for some scholars argued that within the older British and Irish traditions lay traces of a purer form of the law and liturgy as it was laid down by the first councils of the Church. Such forms derived from the close contact that the earliest missionaries to Britain had with the churches of Rome and Gaul at the time of those councils, and from Patrick's organisation of the southern Irish church in a more ancient Roman episcopal tradition, two centuries before Augustine came to Kent.

The energy and independence of the monastic systems, that had been the strength of the church in the north and west of Britain, was becoming a weakness now in the expanding Church, because of the increasing divisions.

Matters came to a head in the growing controversy about the different methods of calculating when Easter should fall each year, the anomalies that had arisen through keeping the feast on different dates having been patiently tolerated in Aidan's time. But the underlying issue, everyone knew, was much wider, and concerned the extent to which the independent customs developed by great monastic founders like Columba could continue to be allowed.

Aidan's successors at Lindisfarne, the Scots Finan and then the Irish Colman, stood firmly by the Irish reckoning of Easter and no argument would move them, and the Northumbrian royal family remained divided because Oswy would not be persuaded by the queen and Alcfrith from loyalty to his Ionan upbringing. Then it happened that in the spring of AD 663 the discrepancy in the dating of Easter was such that while the King was holding the feast according to the custom of Iona, the queen and her followers were still fasting and celebrating Palm Sunday; and so Alcfrith, at the instigation of Wilfrid who saw a way of bringing a satisfactory conclusion to these matters at last, sought audience with his father:

'My Lord,' he said, 'we cannot continue as we are in this matter of the observance of Easter. We are becoming a laughing stock and some who would otherwise seek conversion cannot take the faith seriously. You are the king and your word is law. I beg you to call representatives of both sides together, to listen to their arguments and to make a final judgement.'

The request was warmly supported by Enfleda, for not only was she anxious to see Roman traditions followed but she also knew well that the issue could make good cause for insurrection if Alcfrith was so minded.

'Then let us rid ourselves of this problem once and for all,' said Oswy wearily. 'For myself I am content to go on in the old tradition, and do not see that the matter is so very great and that the feelings of everyone cannot continue to be accommodated within our faith. It is not of such grave account that the queen keeps her celebrations at a different time.' Oswy had never given much thought to the deeper issues involved. 'But to many it seems to be of overriding importance. A synod shall be called, and both sides fairly represented, and I will make a final judgement for the church in Northumbria. Agilbert, bishop of the West Saxons, shall be chief spokesman for the Roman usage, and Colman of Lindisfarne for the Ionan tradition, with others of their choice to support them. It shall be held before the winter sets in, while travel is still possible and the days not yet too short. This will give time enough for preparation. But where shall it be held?'

'Let us put the arrangements into Hilda's hands,' said Enfleda eagerly, 'she will make good and orderly provision, and no-one will mind the simplicity of her fare and accommodation since she will see that everything of importance is thought of. She should herself take part in the council, such is her knowledge now of ecclesiastical matters and so respected her wisdom and justice. Perhaps she herself will be persuaded to see the rightness of the Roman tradition at last, and that would give me the greatest happiness. Let the synod be held at Whitby.'

CHAPTER 8

ilda rose from her knees and left her cell. Beyond the rim of the sea a chill grey light was turning the night sky to iron as, flinging a cloak about her, she began to climb the steep slope beyond the abbey, hoping to find in the high and lonely wilderness of stones that had once been a Roman signal station the calm that would not come in prayer, for she was deeply troubled. Not far from the path candlelight flickered in a shed and she knew that Caedmon, up all night most likely, was tending a sick animal, but she did not pause. The light in the east grew, catching the crests of angry waves far below her as they lashed the desolate cliffs in the first gales of autumn.

God send me humility, send me humble acceptance if the decision goes against us for we have prayed that your will shall be done. I fear the forces ranged against us by those who seek power and wealth either for themselves or for the Church, who do not follow the simple and Christlike life that was the way of Columba and of Aidan, for it is not just the will of God that they are looking for. But I will accept the decision. I will accept it, for the Church must not be divided. Only, dear God, let it be right. Let it be right!

Then below her in the abbey the bell sounded for the first service of the day, and swiftly, with sure sandalled feet she began to descend, and as she passed the cowherd's shed Caedmon came out and stood before her. Caedmon the inarticulate, always so fearful in her presence, stood in her path. And she saw that his face was full of love and pity, pity for her, for Hilda the abbess, and he put out his hand and touched her: yes, touched her as he would a distressed animal. And she looked into his eyes and smiled and went on her way full of wonder, and humility at last, and calm, and a buoyant hope. Why had she been so fearful? She knew how haltingly the Frankish Agilbert spoke, for he had never mastered the Anglo-Saxon tongue and could hold no-one's attention for long. Had not Cenwalh, king of Wessex, replaced him as bishop of Dorchester for that very reason? Agilbert would be no match for Colman.

Tranquilly she led the holy office, and no-one would have guessed at her early turmoil. And the pure antiphons, the blending of male and female voices, calmed her spirit further. Then briskly she checked that everything was prepared; that a long refectory table had been carried into the great meeting hall, that a finely carved chair was placed at its head for the king with another beside it for Alcfrith, and lesser ones for the delegates who would face one another from either side. Benches were placed for the clergy accompanying Colman and for the handful of monks and nuns whom she had chosen to be present from her own community, and there was a low stool in readiness for Elfleda because Hilda wished the child to observe and understand the issues so far as she could. She arranged for the readiness of simple refreshment, in case the council proved long and wearisome. Then she sent young monks to summon from the visitor's quarters those who had rested in the monastery the previous night: Agilbert, bishop of the West Saxons, and his priest Agatho, Enfleda's chaplain Romanus, and James the deacon, companion long ago of Paulinus, old now and full of days and wondering a little why he should be called to discuss matters that had never much concerned him, and just at a time when he was teaching new chants to the choir at York. He smiled across at Hilda with deep affection and a shrug of perplexed apology that he seemed to be opposing her. These took their seats upon the Roman side.

They had been hard put to it, Hilda thought, to find

sufficient support. But there still remained one chair empty, beside Agilbert.

Then Colman, bishop of Lindisfarne, came and took his place as leader on the opposite side. Colman, wise and learned and well-versed to state his case, and accompanied by clergy ready to supply him with passages from scripture and from the fathers that they knew by heart, should his memory falter. Then the venerable Cedd took his seat: Cedd the itinerant bishop of the East Saxons, Anglo-Saxon by birth but educated with his three brothers by Aidan at Lindisfarne. He had made the short journey the previous day from his monastery at Lastingham, ready to interpret and expound questions of doctrine for either side. Hilda sat beside him with her own scholars behind her, and with them the ten-year-old Elfleda, bright eyed and excited, looking eagerly for the arrival of her father and step-brother, her hand held firmly by the nun Begu, who would take her out if she should fidget, though she had promised not to.

Then a messenger came to say that the king approached and the delegates rose to their feet, as, leaving his thanes outside the hall, Oswy entered accompanied by Alcfrith and by the tall monk Wilfrid who had ridden with them on fast horses from York, rising at dawn. So that it appeared as if everyone rose for him too, as he took the empty chair beside Agilbert, and resentment, instantly subdued, rose in Hilda. She looked at him closely as he bent and spoke in a low voice to Agilbert, at the habit of fine cloth that he wore, at the cross and the ring of rare Frankish workmanship, at the curling dark hair, carefully tonsured in the Roman manner, that clustered thickly round his shaven crown. She saw the confidence of his bearing as he spoke to the bishop, and felt an energy emanating from him that set him apart from everyone else. Feeling her watching him he looked up with dark intelligent restless eyes and gave a slight, formal bow. Resentment rose in her again, and a quick apprehension. Young monks in her experience did not look so confident, or so prosperous.

The king gestured to the company to sit down and rose

himself to open the proceedings. He observed that all who served the One God should follow the one rule of life, and since they all hoped for one kingdom in heaven they should not differ in celebrating the sacraments of heaven. The synod now had the task of determining which was the truest tradition, and this should be loyally accepted by all. He then directed his own bishop Colman to speak first, and to explain his own customs and their origin.

Then Colman said: 'The Easter customs which I observe were taught me by my superiors, who sent me here as a bishop; and all our forefathers, men beloved of God, are known to have observed these customs. And lest anyone condemns or rejects them as wrong, it is recorded that they owe their origin to the blessed evangelist Saint John, the disciple especially loved by our Lord, and all the churches over which he presided.'

When he had concluded these and similar arguments, the king directed Agilbert to explain the origin and authority of his own customs.

Agilbert replied: 'May I request that my disciple the priest Wilfrid be allowed to speak in my place? For we are in full agreement with all those here present who support the traditions of our church, and he can explain our position in the Anglo-Saxon language more competently than I can do through an interpreter.'

A stir ran through the company, for had not the venerable Cedd attended for that very purpose? A shock of anger rose in Hilda. Wilfrid looked expectantly towards Oswy who seemed unsurprised by the request and nodded his permission. Then Wilfrid rose and looked from his commanding height upon the assembled company.

'Our Easter customs,' he began in a ringing voice, 'are those that we have seen universally observed in Rome, where the blessed apostles Peter and Paul lived, taught, suffered, and are buried. We have also seen the same customs generally observed throughout Italy and Gaul when we travelled through these countries for study and prayer. Furthermore, we have found them to be observed in many different countries and languages at the same time in Africa, Asia, Egypt, Greece, and throughout the world wherever the Church of Christ has spread. The only people who are stupid enough to disagree with the whole world are these Scots and their obstinate adherents the Picts and Britons, who inhabit only a portion of these two islands in the remote ocean.'

The company gasped. Hilda's face flushed crimson. The elderly James, his mind far away among the sweet lines of the new antiphon, came back to the proceedings with a jerk.

Then Colman answered: 'It is strange that you call our customs stupid when they rest on the authority of so great an apostle, who was considered worthy to lean on our Lord's breast, and whose great wisdom is acknowledged throughout the world.'

Wilfrid replied: 'Far be it from us to charge John with foolishness, for he literally observed the Law of Moses at a time when the Church was still greatly influenced by the synagogue, and the apostles were not able immediately to abrogate the observances of the Law once given by God, lest they gave offence to believers who were Jews (whereas idols on the other hand, being inventions of the devil, must be renounced by all converts). For this reason Paul circumcised Timothy, offered sacrifice in the Temple, and shaved his head at Corinth with Aquila and Priscilla, with the sole intention of avoiding offence to the Jews. For James said to Paul, "You see brother, how many thousands among the Jews have believed, and all of them zealously observe the Law." But today, as the Gospel spreads throughout the world, it is unnecessary and undesirable for the faithful to be circumcised or to offer animals to God in sacrifice. John, following the customs of the Law, used to begin the Feast of Easter on the evening of the fourteenth day of the first month, whether it fell on the Sabbath or on any other day. But Peter, when he preached in Rome, remembering that it was on the day after the Sabbath that our Lord rose from the dead and gave the world the hope of resurrection, realised that Easter should be kept as follows: like John, in accordance with the Law, he waited for moonrise on the evening of the fourteenth day of the first month. And if the Lord's Day, then called the day after the Sabbath, fell on the following day, he began to observe Easter the same evening, as we do today. But if the Lord's Day did not fall on the day following the fourteenth day of the moon, but on the sixteenth, seventeenth, or any other day up to the twenty-first, he waited until that day, and on the Sabbath evening preceding it he began the observance of the Easter Festival. This evangelical and apostolical tradition does not abrogate but fulfil the Law, which ordained that the Passover be kept between the eve of the fourteenth and twenty-first days of the moon of that month. And this is the custom of all the successors of blessed John in Asia since his death, and is also that of the world-wide Church. This is the true and only Easter to be observed by the faithful. It was not newly decreed by the Council of Nicaea, but reaffirmed by it, as church history records. It is quite apparent to us, Colman, that you follow neither the example of John, as you imagine, nor that of Peter, whose tradition you deliberately contradict. Your keeping of Easter agrees neither with the Law nor the Gospel. For John, who kept Easter in accordance with the decrees of Moses, did not keep to the first day after the Sabbath: but this is not your practice; for you keep Easter only on the first day after the Sabbath. Peter kept Easter between the fifteenth and twenty-first days of the moon; you do not, for you keep it between the fourteenth and twentieth days of the moon. As a result, you often begin Easter on the evening of the thirteenth day, which is not mentioned in the Law. Nor did our Lord, the Author and Giver of the Gospel, eat the old Passover or institute the Sacrament of the New Testament to be celebrated by the Church in memory of His Passion on that day, but on the fourteenth. Furthermore, when you keep Easter you totally exclude the twenty-first day, which the Law of Moses particularly ordered to be observed. Therefore I repeat, you conform neither to John nor Peter, the Law nor the Gospel, in your keeping of our greatest Festival.'

The piercing black eyes fixed on Colman, and everyone for a moment was silent, taken aback by the fluency and scholarship of the newcomer, the confidence in the deep musical voice. Then Colman, a little shaken, asked him:

'Do you maintain that Anatolius, a holy man, highly spoken of in church history, taught contrary to the Law and the Gospel, when he wrote that Easter should be kept between the fourteenth and twentieth days of the moon? Are we to believe that our most revered Father Columba and his successors, men so dear to God, thought or acted contrary to Holy Scripture when they followed this custom? The holiness of many of them is confirmed by heavenly signs, and their virtues by miracles; and having no doubt that they are Saints, I shall never cease to emulate their lives, customs and discipline.'

'It is well established that Anatolius was a most holy, learned and worthy man,' answered Wilfrid, 'but how can you claim his authority when you do not follow his directions? For he followed the correct rule about Easter and observed a cycle of nineteen years; but either you do not know of this general custom of the Christian church, or else you ignore it. He calculated the fourteenth day of the moon at Easter according to the Egyptian method, counting it in the evening as the fifteenth day; similarly he assigned the twentieth to Easter Sunday, regarding it after sunset as the twenty-first day. But it appears that you do not realise this distinction, since you sometimes keep Easter before the full moon, that is, on the thirteenth day. And with regard to your Father Columba and his followers, whose holiness you imitate and whose rules and customs you claim to have been supported by heavenly signs, I can only say that when many shall say to our Lord on the day of judgement: "Have we not prophesied in Thy name, and cast out devils, and done many wonderful works?" the Lord will reply, "I never knew you." Far be it from me to apply these words to your fathers, for it is more just to believe good rather than evil of those whom one does not know. So I do not deny that they were true servants of God and dear to Him, and that they loved Him in primitive simplicity. Nor do I think that their ways of keeping Easter were in any way harmful, so long as no-one came to show them a more perfect way. Indeed, I feel certain that if any Catholic reckoner had come to them, they would readily have accepted his guidance, since we know that they readily observed such of God's ordinances as they already knew. But you and your colleagues are most certainly guilty of sin if you reject the decrees of the Apostolic See and the universal Church which are confirmed by these Letters. For although your Fathers were holy men, do you imagine that they, a few men in a corner of a remote island, are to be preferred before the universal Church of Christ throughout the world? And even if your Columba'— Wilfred stopped, suddenly made uncertain by the mounting tension that he sensed opposite to him, and added hastily, 'or, may I say, ours also if he was the servant of Christ — was a Saint potent in miracles, can he take precedence before the most blessed Prince of the apostles, to whom our Lord said: "Thou art Peter, and upon this rock I will build my church, and the gates of hell shall not prevail against it, and to thee I will give the keys of the kingdom of heaven."?'

Wilfrid looked around the silent company and encountered in the grey eyes of the abbess something that disturbed him. It was a look of undisguised fury. For when he had spoken so about Columba the control that she had struggled for was washed away in the tide of anger that flooded her. Hatred surged through her, so that the old pain clutched and knotted her stomach and she held the sides of her chair, fearing that she might fall. And the child Elfleda behind her, enthralled by Wilfrid, whose like she'd never seen, and realising that something that she didn't understand was causing her beloved Mother in God the most acute distress, leaned forward and grasped her hand in a firm hot clasp, before Begu, who was dozing a little, could restrain her.

Wilfrid looked quickly away towards the king. Oswy nodded to him to be seated and turning to Colman asked: 'Is this true, Colman, that these words were spoken to Peter by our Lord?'

Oswy had not followed the arguments relating to Easter, but here was a point that he could understand.

Colman answered: 'It is true, Your Majesty.'

Then the king said: 'Can you show that a similar authority was given to your Columba?'

'No' replied Colman.

'Do you both agree,' the king continued, 'that these words were indisputably addressed to Peter in the first place, and that our Lord gave him the keys of the kingdom of heaven?'

Both answered: 'We do.'

At this the king concluded: 'Then I tell you, Peter is guardian of the gates of heaven and I shall not contradict him. I shall obey his commands in everything to the best of my knowledge and ability; otherwise when I come to the gates of heaven he who holds the keys may not be willing to open them.'

Oswy smiled broadly at his simple and satisfying solution. He was well pleased, for this honourable capitulation simultaneously removed any cause for his son to attempt to depose him. He looked expectantly round the company for their assent. He did not intend further discussion or that the scholars present should begin examining what he had said. He would not call upon the abbess, or anyone else, to speak. The matter was now closed.

One by one they bowed their heads in agreement, the abbess bending so low that none could see her face. Then gently releasing her hand from Elfleda's she rose and gave orders for refreshment to be brought and quickly left the hall.

Elfleda knew that Hilda would go to her cell, there to wrestle with the passion that gripped her. The child longed to comfort her, and to see that she had refreshment, for she knew that it was a long time since she had eaten. Begu was making up for having been asleep with an extreme watchfulness and Elfleda in any case was never permitted to disturb Hilda in her cell. So for a short time she was docile, but then looking up at her attendant asked if she might go to the kitchens and bid some refreshment for the abbess.

'It is a long time since she has eaten,' said Elfleda, 'and I know that she would have something now. Permit me to give the order to the nuns in the kitchen and I will come straight-away back.' She smiled winningly and the nun allowed her to go.

In the kitchen Elfleda enquired as to what was cooking and found that a broth of vegetables and meat was broiling in a bronze skillet and that bread was freshly baked.

'Prepare me a bowlful of the broth and a good piece of bread and with it a cup of mead,' she said to the nun in charge. 'I am to take it to our Holy Mother.'

She spoke imperiously for she had learned this to be useful when she did not wish to be questioned, and soon the food was ready on a large wooden platter and covered with a cloth ready for her to carry to the abbess' cell.

There was no response to Elfleda's gentle knock and she raised the latch and looked timidly inside at the prostrate figure on the pallet, prepared to be rebuked. But Hilda lay weak, drained of all feeling but a great weariness, and indeed the sight of the platter that Elfleda brought was very welcome. The child sat beside her and did not speak, but watched lovingly as she ate, and noted the colour returning to her face. She struggled to hold back the questions that she knew she must keep for a better time, but at last blurted:

'Truly he did not seem to me so very wicked, that Wilfrid, for he believes most sincerely that he is right. And oh, how handsome he is!'

Then the last of the tension ebbed away from Hilda and she laughed her ringing laugh:

Dear God, when will I learn humility? Today the battle has been sore, so sore that I was all but overcome, and you sent to help me first the herdsman and now the child.

She lay back on her pallet and Elfleda knew that she would sleep and crept out and told Begu, who was waiting outside in a state of most acute anxiety, to see that no-one on any account disturbed her.

Colman came next morning to bid the abbess goodbye. He looked into her face with tenderness for he saw that she was full of sadness still.

'Do not grieve for the decision,' he said. 'I think that perhaps it had to be. The Church of Christ grows fast and will soon reach every corner of our island, and in the world beyond the same is happening. It may be that the independence of the old monastic systems must give way to more regular and disciplined ways: that there must be a common liturgy and rule if the Church is to be properly administered. The foundations laid in Iona will remain, and the work of Columba and Aidan never forgotten, but the old ways must change to meet new needs, and above all there must not be division.

'There is room within the Church for both the visionaries and the administrators,' he added quickly, watching the bowed head before him. 'They are necessary and complementary to one another, and in the days to come God will find those who can combine both qualities. Such a one I see already in Cuthbert of Melrose, who will soon go to Lindisfarne as prior. He is an able administrator, but one whose heart yearns for the hermit's life of uninterrupted prayer and study. He did not care for the Roman customs insisted on by Alcfrith for the monastery at Ripon, and left with Eata, who is replaced by Wilfrid. He has returned as prior to Melrose where he is insistent upon strict rule and discipline. I know how irksome he sometimes finds his earthly and material tasks.' Colman looked intently at Hilda. 'You are no stranger to such tensions yourself,' he said, delicately changing the subject.

'Indeed no,' she said, looking up, 'there is never time enough for contemplation, nor for the study that I am in need of. I long for greater skill in the Latin tongue. I understand the scriptures and the fathers passably, but the commentaries are difficult, nor can I translate easily into our own tongue so that those who may one day learn to read can do so without first studying Latin.'

'That must be for others to undertake,' Colman said prophetically. 'Great calls are made upon you and never was a monastery run with such smoothness, such care for all within its walls, as well as such high order of scholarship. It is a

102

pattern for us all. It is well that you are strong, but still you must have a care for yourself and delegate to others when you can.

'For myself I shall resign now from Lindisfarne. This is not because I do not accept Oswy's ruling. I assented to it, and I believe that so it must be. But it is better that I make way for someone with more heart for it. I hope that you too will come to feel reconciled.' He looked at her questioningly.

'You must remember,' she replied, 'That I too assented, for I believe that the decision was God's will so that his Church should not be divided, and I have asked his forgiveness for my sinful grief and anger. I am no stranger to the ways of Augustine's church for it was Paulinus who first taught me and then baptised me. In all the essentials of law and liturgy, and in our study of the gospels, there is no difference of any great importance between us. Yet I believe that those mysteries that are beyond our understanding, Christ's Holy Incarnation and his Resurrection and his promise to us of eternal life, are not to be defined by any dogma that man can devise. They are for each to seek and understand in his own way. And I have come to love the holy life of poverty and prayer, and the saints who have followed it, for that was the way of Christ, and under such obedience God's will is soon made clear and there is little need for the restrictions of rule, when the letter becomes of more importance than the spirit, or for the distractions of outward show and circumstance.'

'I believe that too,' said Colman, and he rose to bid her goodbye, and she drew herself up with dignity, but with the ghost of a smile she added:

'So I will accept the rulings of the Roman church but I shall interpret them as I see fit for the needs of my community here, and in some matters God alone shall be my guide.'

'We may not meet again,' said Colman gently, as she knelt for his blessing, 'but always you will be in my heart, and always I will remember your courage and obedience and thank God for your life and work.'

So Bishop Colman departed for Lindisfarne and there

resigned his bishopric, and he returned to Iona bearing with him some of the sacred bones of Aidan and accompanied by those of his monks who would not fall in with the new ways. Those that remained were persuaded through the patient persistence of their prior, Cuthbert, that they must bow to the synod's decision and accept the customs of Rome, as he had done himself.

Then Alcfrith persuaded Oswy that Wilfrid should be made bishop of York, with power over the whole Northumbrian church. And Wilfrid, dubious of the authority of any bishop in Britain to ordain him, journeyed to Gaul and was consecrated with great splendour at Compiegne by Agilbert, newly appointed as bishop of Paris. Twelve Frankish bishops participated in the ceremony and Wilfrid was carried in triumph to the sanctuary upon a chair of gold.

It was two years before he returned to Northumbria, and in the meantime Alcfrith had lost influence with his father and could no longer help his favourite. Then Oswy grew impatient with waiting for his bishop and appointed Chad, who was brother to Cedd, to take his place at York. Humbly Wilfrid accepted this demotion when he did return, and put his time to good use among his monks at Ripon. He began to introduce there the Rule of St Benedict, made by the saint in the previous century for his monastery at Monte Cassino. Already in use at Canterbury it was as yet unknown in the north of Britain, although it had much in common with the rule that Hilda had devised at Whitby. It brought order and moderation into monastic life, replacing the extremes of austerity that had marked the hermit movement in the East and carried into the Irish church. And Wilfrid sent to Canterbury for two singing masters so that his choir could learn the Gregorian chanting that Augustine had introduced, and the techniques of antiphonal singing such as James the deacon had for many years taught at York.

Patiently and industriously Wilfrid bided his time, confident in God's will to restore him to his former power.

CHAPTER 9

It was early summer in the year AD 669. The monk Edfrith stood beside his work bench in the scriptorium at Whitby looking down upon the vellum sheet upon which he was working. It was the opening page of an illuminated psalter, and he had not before been entrusted with so important a work. It would not be for common use, but to stand upon the altar, and must be of the very finest workmanship so that the people would understand how holy is the word of God. He had already written the column of text in a dense dark ink made from powdered carbon, using the fine formal script that is called insular majuscule, whose use was spreading into Northumbria from the scriptoria of Ireland and Iona. The page was ruled with a grid of faint lines, and pricked with dots in a geometric pattern upon which Edfrith was beginning to draw the complex free-hand design that would decorate the margins and the great capital letter at the beginning of the first verse. Beside him on the bench lay several bone tablets hollowed to hold the layer of wax upon which he had sketched out his plan, a range of styli, some of bronze and some of bone, the quills that he had used for the script, and three or four little palates of brightly coloured pigment. At last milder weather had come, and his every sense was alert and his fingertips tingling as he commenced the delicate drawing. The winter had been long and hard and the spring cold, and his hands always too numbed for anything but the work of preparation. Painstakingly he had scraped both sides of the calf skin for the vellum pages, constantly re-sharpening his knife on a whetstone, until every particle of hair and flesh was removed and the surface white and without blemish, as if it had been polished. And he had sketched out on wax hundreds of studies ready for use in the final design.

He was a young man of remarkable ability both as scholar and artist, who had made his way from Ireland, where he had undergone training already, to Whitby, because of its fast growing reputation as a place of learning. Promised to the Church from an early age, Edfrith had not long since been tonsured as a monk and taken his vows of poverty, chastity and obedience with only a passing thought for the denials that these involved, so sure was he that his calling would lead to the fulfilment of his passion for line and colour, and of the hunger for learning that consumed him.

The monk in charge of the scriptorium watched him with stern interest. Hilda had given instructions, of which he did not altogether approve, that Edfrith should be encouraged to use his talents with unrestricted freedom, for she had been struck by his abilities at once. He moved now to look over the young man's shoulder at the design that was beginning to take shape upon the smooth vellum, carefully positioned to catch the clear morning light.

'You are having a fine time there with the pagan designs from the jewellery workshops,' he said a little sourly. 'Serpents snaking into plant forms that interlock with strange animals and birds, such as no man has seen. Do you think that suitable for a great Christian text?'

'Why yes, father,' said Edfrith with eager respect, 'for I think that the pagan artists have discovered, although they knew nothing of the God who ordained it, a concept that is of great significance; the understanding that in God's plan for the universe every form of life is linked together. It is also a theme in certain of the psalms, and I wish my design to draw out this meaning from them. Christian symbols will weave into the pattern too.'

The master looked uncertain. 'Use those ancient motives with restraint,' he said, 'and tell me when you have planned the colour. You know that some pigments are rare and expensive and we must make enquiries for them at other monasteries, and among travellers to the continent and even to the

East. We may have to ask the Holy Mother for extra funds.' He relented a little. 'I think that will be no problem, when she sees the quality of your work.'

Edfrith flushed with pleasure at the unexpected praise and bent to his work again, and the older man moved on.

A shadow fell across the page and Edfrith looked round and saw that the girl Elfleda was standing against the light behind him.

'Move away a little,' he said curtly, returning to his drawing, 'You take my light.'

Elfleda would soon be fifteen. It was already more than time that she became a novice and before long take her vows, but Hilda had hesitated and would not press it. She felt that the child was not quite ready, and she was reluctant to bring the freedoms of her childhood to a close. She was receiving the best of instruction in the monastery schools and showing great aptitude. Other matters could wait.

Elfleda stepped quickly to one side when Edfrith spoke, but did not go away. The rare colours set out on the bench enchanted her and she had never seen so fascinating a design as the one now before her eyes, although she had been in the scriptorium often and was permitted to watch the monks at work provided that she kept still and silent so that their concentration was not disturbed.

Edfrith became absorbed again and she continued to watch him, amazed by his dexterity and the effortless drawing that flowed from the sharpened charcoal, occasionally interupted so that he could rub away with a soft woollen cloth anything that did not entirely satisfy him. In her interest she moved closer so that inadvertently she stood in his light again and he threw back his head ready to be impatient, but in that moment was aware of her form outlined against the window space; noticed her shape beneath the girdled tunic of fine linen that she wore, and the loveliness of her shadowed face; saw that she was fast becoming a beautiful young woman. She looked back startled at his change of expression from impatience to wonder, for reasons that she did not understand, and blushed deeply for she recognised him then as someone she had observed often of late, so different did he seem from his fellows in a grace and charm of appearance and bearing that the austere trappings of a monk could not disguise. Edfrith looked away hastily and bent low over his task, but reassured by his expression she began in a low voice to ask him questions, eager, searching, that she could no longer contain, forgetting completely that she should not. When would he start using the beautiful colours, and how apply them, and could she come and watch him do it if she kept quiet and still? And how did the drawing flow from his hand so easily? Had he practised it for years? And where did his ideas come from? Had he seen such motifs in other illuminated books or were some of them his own imagination?

Edfrith too forgot that there should be silence in the scriptorium. Delightedly he turned to her, told her how God had given him the gift of great precision in drawing and an understanding of line and form and colour, and that in Ireland he had already had experience in the copying of texts.

'I have come to Whitby,' he said, 'because of the reputation of its teaching under the abbess Hilda, and the importance that she is known to attach to every form of artistic expression. My studies in Latin now enable me to translate and understand the words that I am copying, and to read the commentaries of the fathers.' He paused. 'It brings a new dimension to imagination, for sometimes God shows me the meaning of the text through images and symbols that come unbidden to my mind as I read, so that the illumination becomes part of the understanding of the words themselves, and for others who will look at it too, perhaps.'

He looked at her expectantly. He had not tried to explain this to anyone before, but she understood perfectly what he meant and smiled agreement into his eyes. She moved a finger tip along the interlacing spirals that he had drawn, taking care not to touch the page.

'I could spend happy hours following out the pattern,' she exclaimed. 'I cannot tell where plant becomes animal, and animal bird, and bird fish or snake, for they weave into the whole with tendrils of branch and feather and fin. Oh but the birds especially are beautiful, and each one different!'

'I study the sea-birds here,' he answered, 'in flight, or as they perch in stillness on the rocks, or thrust food into the gullets of their young. And the forms of animals I have studied too, but sometimes strange beasts come to my mind, dragons and reptiles conjured from the stories of our forebears, or that I have seen in jewellery and sculptured stone and in the sacred texts of earlier times and other lands.'

Elfleda was lost in thought. Suddenly she said: 'Caedmon would like to see your designs. He knows about these things: how life, and matter, and season, are linked together.'

'Caedmon?' Edfrith was taken aback. 'The herdsman? How do you know that? He will not speak to anyone. No-one knows his thoughts.'

'Children do,' she answered, 'and animals. To us he tells his thoughts, as well as the old tales, now that he has come to understand our tongue and can speak it.'

She asked him how he would decide upon his colours, and how mix them, and he explained how the white of egg was used, or sometimes a glue made from fish bones, and how the colours could be blended to make different shades. He showed her the colours that he had there, red and white lead, yellow ochre and verdigris, and woad and a range of pinks and purples made from specially cultivated plants. He told her how he hoped that for the illumination of the great capital letter he might obtain a little of the crimson pigment called kermes, and some indigo, and rare lapis lazuli, that came from lands in the East. He explained how the red dots that he so favoured were there not just as outline but to soften the effect of colour against the white vellum.

Oblivious now to everything else, to who and where they were, they conversed with increasing understanding and delight in one another's company. The monk in charge had gone, and the other monks, absorbed in their copying in another part of the scriptorium for some time did not notice the low murmur of conversation, but after a while they began to look up in surprise and at last one of them went to find

Begu. He bid her fetch away the girl at once and watch her more carefully, and then admonished Edfrith to have a care.

They were never to speak to one another again. Only sometimes their eyes met as they chanced to pass, glanced with quick yearning and looked away. Then a strange restlessness filled Elfleda. The imperious wilfulness that she had learned to subdue returned, countered by bursts of extravagant generosity and affection, and storms of tears. Edfrith returned to his work on the psalter with passionate energy, working until his eyes ached and his back and his hands were seized by painful cramps. His design no longer satisfied him, and leaving the vellum page carefully covered with a cloth he began to draw, on fresh wax tablets, a new one with ever more fanciful motifs ingeniously and voluptuously intertwined. The master watched him, and at last spoke angrily:

'You must control yourself, Edfrith,' he said. 'That is fit for no Christian text. It is too passionate, all but lewd indeed. Scrape the tablet clear now, and start again if you must, though there is nothing wrong with your first design.'

'Do not, do not ask me to destroy it,' pleaded the young man, 'for it is beautiful, my very best, I know it. It is a deeper understanding of the text that has been vouchsafed me, and it is Truth.'

A long shadow fell between them. It was the abbess who stood behind them, her hand stretched out towards the tablet.

'It must not be destroyed,' she said gently to the master. She turned to Edfrith and looked into his distraught face with deep compassion.

'It is beautiful,' she said, 'and the best you have yet done, but perhaps not suitable for the opening of a psalter. It must be carefully stored.' She smiled. 'One day you must illuminate the Song of Solomon.'

In the next weeks Hilda watched in anxious love over the daughter that God had given into her keeping, and over the gifted young monk. Then late one afternoon she made opportunity to climb with Elfleda to the clifftop and they sat together in a sunlit patch of moorland. There was a heavy silence between them. Only the waves whispered against the pebbles far below, and the pollen-laden bees murmured among the opening buds of heather.

'Edfrith has gone,' said Hilda at last, 'to Lindisfarne. It is for his sake, as well as for yours. His gifts must be protected, at whatever the cost, and besides he has taken his vows. Your own great gifts must not be squandered either.'

She did not look at the girl, who had turned away from her.

'It was a hard promise that was made for you,' she continued. 'It is a hard vow that you will make, but only sometimes. It is only sometimes that the yearning is very great, and the joy and the freedom of being dedicated, unfettered, to God, make it a small price to pay. You can work for him in a way that is denied to those with the ties of the flesh.'

But this was too hard for Elfleda. She tried to speak but could not, for she was weeping bitterly now, and her face was buried in the lap of her Holy Mother.

'Don't try to speak,' said Hilda, her hand caressing the bright hair. 'I know what you are trying to say. You are free. You have not taken your vows. There might be ways of foreswearing Oswy's promise. But it could never be Edfrith, a tonsured monk with a sure vocation. You know that very well. The time has come now that you must think long and earnestly about your own vows. I will not try to persuade you. If it is more than you can bear I will speak to the king, and to Enfleda your mother.' She stopped. Elfleda was quiet now. Then she said in a low voice, carefully controlled:

'I know that it could never be Edfrith.' She paused, to contain herself again. 'Tell me about the estate of Holy Virginity,' she said.

'It is a high estate,' said Hilda quietly, 'made holy by the Mother of God herself, though in that there lies a mystery whose meaning must be hidden from us in this life. It arose from St Paul's advocation of a life of continence, and was encouraged by the early fathers, by Tertullian and Cyprian and then by Ambrose and Jerome. It was a part of the

111

movement for asceticism, and the idea that all earthly desires are polluting, that was followed by the first Christian anchorites. You know well that I cannot countenance the extremes that derive from this movement, and that in my rule I have respect for the needs of the body. But the calling to religious life comes only to a few, and cannot be fulfilled without the vow of chastity and the freedom that it gives from the demands of earthly ties. In this particular I believe that St Paul and the fathers were right.'

They sat in silence then until the sun began to sink, and dusk fell, and in silence they descended to the monastery.

But Elfleda could find no rest that night and tossed and turned upon her pallet so that Begu, who slept near to her, told her impatiently to be still and sleep. Begu would be thankful to give up her charge, and thought it high time that Elfleda became a novice, but she continued her loving care of the girl in patience, because of her devotion to the holy abbess.

The night was very warm and close, and Elfleda could no longer endure the heat of her thick straw pallet with its covering of woven wool. She left it and lay down upon the floor, laying her hot cheek against the cool beaten earth. She tried to pray but could not. Never had she felt so deserted, so alone. She rose and paced about the small cell and at last stood still in the doorway, breathing deeply of the cooler air outside. Begu came to her side and tried to coax her to lie down again, and when she would not placed a mantle round her shoulders, but Elfleda shook it aside impatiently and told the gentle nun to return to her bed, so that she at least might sleep. Then dawn came, and soon the bell for Nones, followed by soft sandalled footfall, and Elfleda drew back within the doorway as the grey forms of monks and nuns glided from their separated cells to the church, for the first office of the day.

Beyond the satin rim of the sea the stars were fading as the clear sky flushed with light. Begu was breathing heavily in sleep and Elfleda could stay where she was no longer and slipped out, through the rampart that circled the monastery

112

buildings, and down the hillside to a rough track that led to the sea.

Shining day has come now. The world is new-born, washed in white light after the black night. The gleaming pebbles, foam-fresh from the falling tide, pale in the warmth of the rising sun. Flowers open for the first time among the meadow grass that grows behind the shore line, and the dews of night have washed blade and leaf and petal to a crystal clearness. The dawn wind has died away. The sea is like glass, with scarcely a ripple, and Elfleda can see down, down to where the swaying fronds of seaweed are at anchor, down to where the roots of the land lie hidden in the springs of the sea. It is permitted that she sees it all, in a moment of timeless union. Then a cloud drifts over the face of the sun and the brightness falls away and ripples break the surface of the sea. Elfleda sinks to the hard ground, chilled and exhausted. But peace has come, and a calm from that epiphany that will never leave her but stay in her depths to sustain her, as the deeps of the sea are sustained against the storms that cross the surface.

Soon she rose to her feet and made her way back up the rough track and passed within the monastery enclosure.

Hilda had seen her go; knew her turmoil; dared not guess the outcome. Now she saw her come back; saw the radiance of her face despite its weariness; fell upon her knees for she knew that everything was well.

So Elfleda cut off her beautiful hair, so that the nun's wimple would better cover her head, and took the veil, and would be numbered among the Church's greatest abbesses; would be friend and counsellor of Wilfrid and of Cuthbert; would be one in whom the traditions of Rome and of Ireland met in synthesis, when in the course of time she followed her Holy Mother as abbess of Whitby.

And Edfrith went to Lindisfarne and before the century was out became its bishop, and made the great Gospel book that is a miracle of one man's workmanship, and by more miracles has survived the centuries so that it may still be seen.

In this same year of AD 669 the great scholar Theodore of Tarsus was consecrated in Rome as archbishop of Canterbury. He came to Britain accompanied by the abbot Hadrian to assist him in his teaching, and by Benedict Biscop who had made his first visit to Rome with Wilfrid and who returned now to Northumbria, soon to become founder of the monasteries of Wearmouth and Jarrow. These men brought fresh impetus of learning to the monasteries, with a transfusion of books and scholarship from Italy, Spain and Gaul. Then Theodore reinstated Wilfrid as archbishop of York, deposing Chad who humbly accepted the justice of the decision and retired to Lastingham, but for a brief time only because Theodore found that Christianity was growing fast among the Mercian people and consecrated Chad as their first bishop, with his see at Lichfield. And Cuthbert, as prior at Lindisfarne, kept to the traditions of Ireland in the ascetic life that he led and in his missionary journeys among the still barbarous people, but insisted that his monks accept the Roman ruling, and worked patiently to persuade those who remained obstinate that ecclesiastical order was essential now for the future of the growing Church.

The following year Oswy died naturally upon his bed, an end unusual for an Anglo-Saxon king, and Egfrid his son, borne to him by Enfleda and so brother to Elfleda, succeeded him. And Enfleda was free of her divided loyalties at last and entered the monastery at Whitby, where she had so often longed to be.

114

CHAPTER 10

Caedmon the herdsman could not rid himself of his fear of the abbess Hilda, that rendered him tongue-tied in her presence if ever she tried to converse with him. There had been that moment, early in the morning before the Synod was held, when he had overcome it, had indeed been unaware of it and had stretched out his hand to touch her, because of the great need that he knew in her as a creature in distress. But afterward he had returned to his habitual avoidance of her; and yet he watched her still, with loving concern, for he saw that sometimes she grew very weary, and drawn, as if she had been ill.

It was true that there were times when Hilda felt discouraged and at her wits end as to how to bring a true understanding of the faith to the still barbarous tribes-people, so that their minds could be freed from the dread superstitions that clouded them and forced them to accept the poverty of their lives with such fatalism. Often they were openly hostile to the missionaries who went among them, and jeered at the deprivations that the monks appeared to inflict upon themselves when they had no need to, and implored them not to try to rob them of the old religion and impose a new one that they could in no way understand. Hilda cared as deeply for these people as she did for the faithful, for the monks and nuns who worshipped and studied under her rule, and the baptised lay people.

Caedmon too carried a burden. It was some time now since he had been baptised into the faith along with others of the lay brothers who worked on the monastery lands. He was growing old, and still God would not release the gift that

115

was in him: the weight of gold that would not come to birth: folded pinions that would not open.

One day as Hilda paced beside the monastery rampart, deep in thought about the matters that so troubled her, it happened that she saw Caedmon about his tasks on the adjoining farm, and something prompted her to move quickly through the gateway and detain him. She placed a firm hand upon his arm so that this time he could not escape her and he stood still, obediently, but turned his head away so that he did not encounter the pleading in her eyes.

'Caedmon,' she said, 'I do not know what to do. I cannot find words that will bring those of our people who obdurately remain heathen to any true understanding of Christianity, and I think sometimes that such words do not exist, that there comes a point where language fails. Do you understand what I mean, Caedmon?' She looked anxiously, desperately, towards him and he nodded vigorously but still he would not look at her, but stood tense, his head bowed, waiting to be allowed to go. She did not know what to do. She saw his fear and regretted that she had imposed her will on him.

'Help me, Caedmon,' she said, and quickly turned away from him and went back inside the monastery and Caedmon returned to his work, and when he was at a safe distance he looked back and saw her, a stooping lonely figure returning with weary steps along the path that led to her cell.

It was the time for a night of feasting. A time when the people forgot the arduous labour of their days and the hard conditions of their lives and joyed in one another's company; in rustic mirth, in music and dancing, and the telling of the old tales that were held fast in the memory by the rhythm of the long alliterative lines used by the bards who sang or told them. The farmworkers and folk from the village had gathered in the great barn of the monastery farm. They sat upon long benches against the timbered walls; ale was passed round in jugs of coarse pottery, and in the middle of the reed-strewn floor a fire of logs was lit, the blue smoke escaping through the hole cut in the thatch above it. The space round the fire was left empty, ready for a visiting bard, or if none came for the company to entertain one another in turn, with harp or song or story.

Caedmon took his accustomed place in a corner where he did not attract notice. He was a familiar figure to everyone, an eccentric who shunned human contact and lavished care upon every other living thing, but held in affectionate tolerance because of his skill in husbanding the livestock on the farm. At the feasts the people mostly left him alone now and no longer teased him to take his turn, knowing that he would not. Only the reeve, the herdsman in charge of stock and Caedmon's master, sometimes still chided him. He was a bluff man, kindly, but often quick-tempered and impatient, and this night had taken freely of the ale as it passed round. Red-faced now, aggressive and looking for some mischief, his eye fell on Caedmon, deep in the shadows.

'Come now, Caedmon,' he shouted to him, 'Come out of the shadows! Stop hiding there and take your turn with the rest! Give us the story that I heard you whispering to the milking cow this morning. It kept her quiet enough. It might do the same for this noisy company here!'

There was loud laughter, and cheers, though some of those present sought to restrain the reeve when they saw that he would drag Caedmon into the space beside the fire. But Caedmon had seen his intention too, and muttering to those near him that it was his turn to be with the beasts in the stable that night he ducked quickly out through the doorway and into the night, and one or two voices called shame upon the reeve for alarming the gentle herdsman, and just when everyone hoped that he might one day give them some verses if they left him alone for long enough.

It is blackest night. The moon and the stars are hidden and the sky heavy, so that a great weight bears down upon Caedmon; the weight of the universe, the weight of the gift within him that he can no longer carry, that must come to birth if it is not to crush and destroy him. Bent double, groping blindly for the pathway to the stable, he at last reaches it and sinks thankfully into the straw beside the animals. Disturbed by the movement they turn their heads

117

towards him and watch him with drowsy impenetrable eyes, and the sound and rhythm of their breathing brings him an unfathomable calm, so that he falls into a deep sleep.

Then it is that, in a dream, a man stands beside him and calls him by name.

'Caedmon,' he says, 'Sing me a song.'

'I don't know how to sing,' he replies. 'It is because I cannot sing that I left the feast here.'

The man who addresses him then says, 'But you shall sing to me.'

'What shall I sing about?' answers the herdsman.

'Sing about the creation of all things,' says the other.

And Caedmon immediately begins to sing verses in praise of God the creator that he has never heard before, for they come from the deeps of his own being in words of great beauty and power. They are in the Anglo-Saxon tongue that he has mastered now, and in the verse forms he has learned from listening to the bards. Their theme is this:

> It is meet that we should worship the warden of heaven
> The might of the maker his purpose of mind
> The glorious father's work when of all his wonders
> Eternal God made a beginning
> He earliest established for earth's children
> Heaven a roof. Holy shaper
> Then mankind's warden created the world
> Eternal monarch making for men
> Land to live on. Almighty Lord!

When Caedmon awoke he remembered everything that he had sung in his dream, and he began to add more verses in the same style to the glory of God, for the gift remained upon him.

Early in the morning he went to his master, the reeve, and told him about this gift that he had received. The reeve was ashamed that he had seemed to bully the good herdsman at the feast and was glad to make amends, and besides it was very apparent that the man had received a vision.

'We must go to the abbess at once,' he said. Caedmon

118

started in alarm, then bowed his head in agreement. He knew that he must go to her.

Before the reeve could knock upon the door of Hilda's cell the watchful Begu, hearing footsteps, emerged from her own cell that stood close beside it and that she had once shared with Elfleda, and stood squarely against the abbess's closed door. Begu worked among the nuns in the weaving workshop, now that Elfleda had entered the house of the novices, and was skilled in making the undyed woollen twill that was used for the habits of both monks and nuns. But she had pleaded to remain near Hilda so that she could continue to serve her, and with humility Hilda had allowed this care and indeed was grateful for it, although she thought it an indulgence.

'I must see the abbess at once,' said the reeve.

'No,' replied Begu. 'It is not allowed. It is the time that she devotes to study and to prayer. And besides, she is not well. Sometimes now a fever attacks her and leaves her weak.' Begu could never resist a little gossip and passed on such information against Hilda's will.

'All the same I must see her,' replied the reeve, deliberately raising his voice. 'This man has had a vision.'

Begu had not at first noticed Caedmon, standing partly hidden behind the stalwart figure of the reeve. She hesitated, for she knew of Hilda's interest in the herdsman, as she knew many things that concerned the beloved Mother. She did not understand this interest, for she thought the man uncouth, but she knew that Hilda would care very much that he had come to her. But Hilda had heard the loud voice of the reeve and in that moment raised the latch and stood in the doorway.

'Mother,' the reeve said quickly, thrusting Caedmon forward, 'I beg you to see this man. He has had a vision.'

Hilda grasped at the wooden doorpost and lent against it, for she was weak, and Begu ran to support her, but she quickly collected herself. What could have happened to make the herdsman come to her of his own will? Was this another miracle? Would she never learn that God would always show

119

her the way at last, if only she would have patience and humility and wait upon his will?

Caedmon stood still, timid, turned to stone, but he looked into her eyes.

'Leave us now,' she said to the reeve. 'You were right to bring him at once.' She looked at Caedmon with love. 'I hope it was not hard to persuade him,' she said gently.

'No,' said Caedmon, 'I had to come to you, Mother.'

She drew him into the cell and made him sit down beside her. Then he told her all that had happened in the night, haltingly at first but soon the words poured out. He told her of the glory that had been locked within him, his understanding of the world and its Creator that he could not bring to birth in poetry, for he could not find the words and the rhythms as he knew God meant that he should, so that others might share those things that he had come to know. He told her how this had become a burden too great for him to bear, and how he had begun to fear that he would die with his gift stillborn.

Hilda sighed. 'It is very hard to wait upon God's will in patience,' she said. 'For myself it is the hardest of all lessons. But it is never too late. I am growing old too, Caedmon, and impatient that I cannot bring those who so stubbornly resist it to the faith before I die. Now I can see a way, through the songs that you will make for the unlettered people, that shall make the scriptures sing for them and for the generations to come, conjuring an understanding that is far beyond the means of ordinary language. It is a gift that God bestows on very few. And He will give us the years that are necessary. I know this in my heart and your coming has shown it to me yet again. But still I do not learn to be patient.'

He looked at her speechless, amazed that she should share his own anxieties, and that in coming to her he had eased a burden that she carried too.

Then she went on, more briskly, 'Caedmon, we must waste no more time. There is so much to be done, now that we know the way ahead. But first, can you remember your poem, and will you speak it for me?'

120

Caedmon did not hesitate. The words that he had sung in his dream, and the verses that he had added after his awakening, flowed without effort from his memory.

Hilda knew at once that here was a precious and a priceless gift. She did not wish to alarm him, but knew that she must consult with others; that her leading scholars must listen to his account and hear his poem and decide upon its origin and quality, so that they might advise her about the wisest course of action. She asked him gently if he would consent to appear before these learned men and women. But Caedmon no longer felt any fear. The burden had fallen. The wings were unfolding.

All those summoned to hear him agreed that Caedmon's was a gift from God, but they wished to test how it might best be put to use, so they explained to him a certain passage of scripture that people found great difficulty in understanding, and the doctrine derived from it, and asked him to put it into verse. He promised to do so, and returned the next day with verses that astonished them. The words themselves were simple, and such as the common people used, but they were strung together like jewels upon a chain of gold, each one skilfully chosen and placed for its assonance in relation to its neighbours, and ordered in lines that beat with a haunting rhythm. And even those learned scholars who had already studied the passage began to see in it levels of meaning that had never before occurred to them.

Then Hilda advised Caedmon that he should abandon secular life and enter the monastery as a brother, and when he showed some reluctance in leaving his charge of the animals to others she arranged that he could continue to oversee their welfare, for it was part of her rule that monks and nuns must share in secular tasks. And she arranged for him to receive special instruction in the events of sacred history, and he stored in his memory everything that he learned, turning it over again and again in his mind until he could come to the heart of it and give it words, so that its meaning was in its form and its form a part of its meaning.

121

The process, he told the abbess, reminded him of his beasts who so long and patiently chewed upon the cud.

He sang for the people the whole story of Genesis so that they could now properly understand the creation of the world and the origin of the human race, for this was a theme that exercised the hearts of men and was falsely told in the stories of the pagan gods. He sang about the pattern that he had seen in the seasons and in the cycle of birth and death upon the earth, and in the ebb and flow of the salt streams of the sea and in the pathways of the sun and moon across the heavens. He sang of Israel's departure from Egypt and their entry into the land of promise, of their kings and heroes, and of God's unceasing care for his chosen people. He sang of the Lord's Incarnation, Passion, Resurrection and Ascension into heaven, the coming of the Holy Spirit, and the teaching of the apostles. He made poems about the blessings and judgements of God, about the Last Judgement and the horrible pains of Hell, and the joys of the Kingdom of Heaven.

Then Caedmon, who held all matter sacred, who reverenced ancient stone and touched with healing fingers the white wounds of the saplings hewn in the forest, began to ponder deeply upon the Cross of Christ. He thought about its substance, about the wood from which it had been fashioned, stem and branch of living tree grown and watered in the land of Palestine. He thought how it had suffered: mute victim that must not break or bend against God's will to save Him: nails piercing its own fibres: spear thrust wounding to its heart. Might it come to him in dream, angel-borne in glory now of gold and glancing gems, enter the long watches of his night and tell him how it was? Then he would make for the Cross his greatest poem of all, to celebrate the part that it was made to bear, to sing the story of its Passion.

Caedmon waited patiently. One day, before he died, the vision and the words might come.

122

CHAPTER 11

ilda was glad to welcome the widowed queen Enfleda to Whitby, following Oswy's death. Well schooled during her upbringing in Kent in the far-seeing laws that her grandfather Ethelbert had instituted for his kingdom, Enfleda had been an able administrator of the court and kingdom of Northumbria after her marriage to its king. Hilda permitted that she was very soon clothed and blessed as a nun after only a nominal period as novice, because of the devout life that she had led and her long and earnest study of the scriptures. The bouts of burning fever that the abbess had for sometime suffered racked her now continuously. She was fifty-six years old and she began to think that she might die before Elfleda had the authority to take her place. She saw that Enfleda might succeed her as abbess until Elfleda was ready, or that mother and daughter might rule jointly for a period.

The monastery was growing fast. Scholars from far and wide were joining it, and monks were brought in to make missionary journeys among the more distant tribespeople and to care for the sick and poor. New cells were built to accommodate them, fashioned now from stone because the builders were learning the skills of cement-making, lost long ago with the withdrawal of the Roman legions, from the Gaulish builders employed at Ripon and York. The time would soon come for the founding of a sister house, and Hilda had in mind for the site the beautiful wooded valley today called Hackness, served by the little port of Scarborough that lies twenty miles to the south of Whitby. It was easily reached by a broad moorland track marked by the stone cross that Edwin had raised to the memory of his brave thane Lilla. The nun Frigyth, who had followed Hilda from Hartlepool to Whitby and who in everything was her right hand and deputy, would be its first abbess. In this way Frigyth would not be passed over when Enfleda and Elfleda succeeded herself. And the new monastery would make provision for Begu. She should start a weaving workshop there. The devoted nun must begin a new life, though she might not wish it. She was too much concerned for Hilda and would be left desolate when she died. Hilda's mind was continually working on these matters, so that her work would continue uninterrupted by her death.

She knew that when this time came there must be change. In Elfleda the traditions of Iona met and merged with those of Rome, but Enfleda had closer links with the court of Canterbury and held uncompromisingly to Roman customs. And the presence of the royal ladies brought a new prestige to the monastery of Whitby, for it became the burial place of kings. Oswy was buried there at his queen's request, with royal ceremony, beside the altar of the principle church that was dedicated to St Peter, and later Enfleda requested that the bones of her father Edwin were brought from the battlefield of Hatfield and given fit burial there, to the south of the altar and east of a new altar dedicated to St Gregory. And the bodies of others of the royal line were disinterred and brought to Whitby. Elfleda fully shared her mother's royal consciousness, and Hilda, though she no longer herself regarded such matters as important, knew that this must be so. She did not forget her own youth when Edwin had instilled into her the pride of her godlike ancestry, and she remembered how she had often used it to advantage in her care of the people.

The abbess accepted with tranquillity the changes that must come about. She had never wished for a divided Church and after Oswy's decison at the Synod had obediently implemented Roman usages. They did not greatly alter her own observances: the seven services of the divine daily office, the psalms and hymns of the Roman canon that James the deacon

124

had so long ago taught her to love, she had always most faithfully followed in accordance with the practice of the universal Church. Yet she felt that there were areas of theology too full of mystery to be defined, that must be left open to many interpretations, and in these she did not insist upon the dogmas of Rome. And she firmly retained her insistence upon a simple and austere life of labour and study and the holding of all property in common. There was no outward show of finery in her churches or in the trappings of those who administered their services. Only the music, and the fine carving of the stone crosses in the precincts, and now Caedmon's poetry, exalted the understanding of the people. In these ways Hilda held firmly to the traditions of Iona, and of Lindisfarne where her monastery had close contacts by way of well-trodden moorland tracks and a short sea route if the weather was good.

At Lindisfarne Cuthbert had for some years been prior, under its abbot, Eata. He had given up Irish usages himself and worked with extraordinary patience to persuade those of his monks who obstinately refused to abandon their old customs that the new rule that he had introduced must hold, for the sake of an undivided Church. Yet he held very dear to the traditions of poverty and asceticism; living with the utmost frugality, denying himself rest so that he might pray continuously, driving away the heaviness of sleep when it threatened to overcome him with the manual labour that he insisted upon sharing with his monks. He continued his missionary journeys, sometimes on horseback but often on foot, to remote parts of the diocese, making no provision for himself, knowing that God would provide for him as he had for Elijah in the wilderness. He took only his portable altar which was a slab of oak carved with crosses at the four corners and the centre, and a finely shaped and gilded chalice for use with it, made for him in the monastery workshops. In the scriptorium his monks made a small travelling mass book bound in leather. It contained chosen extracts from the canon of the mass gospels, and special prayers for use with

125

the offices of baptism and burial and at the giving of extreme unction.

God had given to Cuthbert great gifts of preaching and teaching, and of prophecy and healing, and a charm that made the people flock to him. Quick in sympathy and compassion, so that he wept for the weak and with the penitent, yet he did not hesitate to call the wrath of God upon wrong-doers. Stories of his miracles circulated far and wide, and it was said that his prayers would restore sufferers from every kind of affliction, even from afar, and that he cured those vexed with unclean spirits through the touch of his hands and by exhortation and exorcism. But he longed to end his days in the solitude that he loved, and in the year AD 676 he gave up his office as prior, and withdrew to the retreat that Aidan had made for himself on the island of the Inner Farne. Here with the help of his monks he built himself a dwelling, circular in plan and with an oratory beside it. It was made from the rough stone and peat dug from its enclosure, with high walls so that he could only see the sky and would not be distracted, and roofed with straw and timber. At the centre of the enclosure he dug a well that filled at once with fresh spring water and neither flooded nor dried out, and the sea supplied him with driftwood if he needed it for any purpose. When the dwelling was finished he sent the monks away and as time went by he withdrew out of sight, within the hermitage, when people sought to visit him and bring him bread, and only sometimes would consent to converse with them through a window.

Barley that he planted for his needs miraculously flourished, and the birds who began to devour it as it ripened obediently flew away at his command. Indeed birds and animals had always been his friends. Ravens who persisted in tearing straw from his thatch returned in contrition after he had angrily driven them off, bringing him a lump of pigs lard as a penitential gift. And it was told by a monk of Coldingham how he had watched the saint, who was at the time visiting the abbess Ebba there, walk into the sea at dead of night and stand up to his neck in water, keeping vigil

126

through the remaining hours of darkness; and how when he returned and knelt upon the sand at daybreak two otters bounded from the waves and stretched themselves beside his frozen feet, warming them with their breath and rubbing dry his body on their fur. Their task done he blessed them and they slipped back into the sea.

Cuthbert's monks could do little for his welfare. It was only once a year at Easter-time, they said, at the ceremonial Washing of the Feet in church on Maundy Thursday, that he would consent to change his boots, and on his shins they found thick callouses of great size where the leather had chafed as he prayed and genuflected.

And still, despite the remoteness of his retreat, the people flocked to see him.

There were other great ecclesiastics in the years following Oswy's death, moderates like Cuthbert who were ready to compromise so that the Church could speak with one authoratative voice: Chad, bishop of the Mercians in the new see of Lichfield; Eata, Abbot of Lindisfarne and later its bishop, a man of wisdom whose acceptance of the Synod's decision helped considerably towards the unity of the Church in Northumbria: Ceolfrith, a Northumbrian monk ordained priest by Wilfrid at Ripon, who travelled for further study first to Canterbury and then in the year AD 670 to Icanhoe in East Anglia where the monk Botulf, who so many years before befriended Hilda's mother Bregusyth, had founded a monastery of great reputation on his return from the Gaulish monastery of Chelles, where Hilda once so nearly went to join her sister Hereswith. Ceolfrith returned to Ripon after his studies. A man of great humility he undertook there the office of baker and in the midst of his duties of sifting flour, lighting and cleaning the oven, and baking loaves, did not forsake his great learning and made time to continue it. Soon he left Ripon for the new monastery of Wearmouth, invited by its founder, Benedict Biscop, and became its prior and introduced there the rule of St Benedict that he had learned at Ripon from Wilfrid.

But Wilfrid was another matter. He saw no need for

compromise and scorned the traditions of Columba and of Aidan. After his reinstatement by archbishop Theodore in the year before Oswy's death he became a figure of great power in the kingdom, in secular as well as in ecclesiastical matters. At York he lavishly restored the stone basilica, fallen into neglect, that Edwin had started to build, and from his seat there he ruled the church throughout Northumbria. Many monasteries named him heir to their possessions in return for his patronage and protection, and he acquired estates throughout the land. His household was famous as a school for training young noblemen in military skills, and he maintained close links with the royal court, and became, after Oswy's death, spiritual adviser to Egfrid's queen, Etheldreda, a daughter of Anna, king of the East Angles.

Etheldreda, many years older than her husband and married to him for political reasons, wished to become a nun and made it a condition of her marriage that she should remain a virgin, and when Egfrid some years later wished to change this state of affairs she was encouraged and supported in its continuation by Wilfrid; a situation that did not endear him to the king. In the year AD 672 Etheldreda was veiled as a nun by Wilfrid at Coldingham, and a year later she founded the double monastery of Ely where she lived an austere life of penance and prayer, and encouraged other noblewomen of her family to join her. To Wilfrid she gave a site at Hexham where he founded a great monastery with a massive church of stone, the finest to be seen anywhere north of the Alps it was said.

Hilda could not forgive Wilfrid for the arrogance, as she considered it, that had swayed Oswy's decision at the Synod, and for his dismissiveness of Columba and the traditions that she had come to love so much. She was further angered now by reports of his great wealth and power, and by his sway over so vast a diocese when there were priests in her own monastery ready to take high office in the church. But Elfleda, who had not forgotten the impression that he made upon her as a child, and who learned of his great gifts from visiting scholars, remained his champion.

'Mother,' she pleaded with Hilda, whom she visited whenever her duties as a novice allowed, 'his possessions and his power are put to the service of the Church and the Church alone, never for himself. The young noblemen placed in his charge become Christian rulers as well as the fine soldiers that they have to be. His own life is austere, with long hours spent in work and study. He is not tempted at the feasts held at his court, and is always temperate. In prayer and vigil, in spiritual reading and in fasting, it is said that he has no equal. And he has humility. He did not seek to depose Chad when he returned from consecration in France and found him made bishop in his place, but returned to Ripon and worked ceaselessly in building his noble church there to the glory of God, and in teaching and training his monks.'

Hilda smiled wryly. 'There was nothing very humble about the dedication ceremony of the new church at Ripon,' she said, 'or about the sumptuous altar hangings that he had commissioned for it, and the illuminated Gospel Book written in gold upon purple parchment with a gold and jewelled binding. And it was said that in the presence of the king and of the whole royal court he read aloud, with great circumstance, all the royal charters which have endowed Ripon with land.'

'But it was done that God might be glorified in the eyes of the people,' insisted Elfleda. 'His lands create great wealth for the Church, so that it can care better for the sick and poor, and build up libraries and provide education and found more monasteries. Wilfrid believes that fine buildings and music and treasure must be put to the service of God, so that the people may see that nothing is too precious, too costly, for his service.'

Hilda looked away, deeply troubled. 'It is not the simple life that Christ led,' she said, 'and that Aidan and Columba followed. Nor does it accord with the traditions of the Roman church set out by Pope Gregory and brought by Augustine to Canterbury. Gregory advocated a monastic life of simplicity, with all possessions held in common. He condemned the display of power and wealth. You know this, for you

129

rightly admire and study the writings of Gregory and have learned from your mother the traditions taught by Augustine that she knows so well, and that were taught to me too, by Paulinus. Wilfrid has found this concern for possessions and outward circumstance, that so tunes with his own inclinations, in his contacts with the Gaulish bishops, who are of the nobility and powerful landowners. It is not part of the Roman tradition as we know it. His power has grown too great, and he cannot manage so great a diocese alone. There are priests here in our monastery who would bring learning of a high order, and long experience in ecclesiastical matters, into the life of the Church if high office could be found for them. Hedda will soon be consecrated by Theodore as bishop to the West Saxons, but Oftor, John and Bosa remain, and the young priest who bears the same name as the bishop, Wilfrid, shows great promise. Besides, concern with such worldly matters becomes corrupting. I have seen it happen too often in the lives of kings and noblemen greedy for wealth and power. And it is a cause of jealousy. You know that already your brother, the king, looks with fear and envy at Wilfrid's temporal power.'

'It is more for other reasons that Egfrid hates Wilfrid,' answered Elfleda straightly. 'It is because Etheldreda would not consummate their marriage when he wanted to retract the undertaking that he had made to her, and he knew that Wilfrid supported her in her wish to remain a holy virgin for Christ's sake, and himself blessed her as a nun when Egfrid agreed at last to let her go.'

'She denied the sacred vows of marriage and was greatly at fault,' exclaimed Hilda angrily. 'There was time for the monastic life when she had borne and raised the king's heirs and carried out her duties as queen. There cannot be virginity and marriage. You know it very well, for you chose between the two yourself. Many queens have taken the veil, though it could not be as holy virgins. Your own mother is such a one, and so was Ethelburga your grandmother, and my sister Hereswith who entered the monastery at Chelles when the sons she had born the East Anglian king were of age and her husband dead.'

'But Holy Virginity is the higher state,' returned the girl, 'and Egfrid agreed to the queen's wish at the time of their marriage. Wilfrid only supported her in following her true vocation when the king changed his mind.'

'Then Wilfrid's was an even greater fault!' Hilda was pale with fury and rounded on Elfleda. 'He had great influence with the queen and misused it. It was in his power to show her where her duty lay and insist that she fulfilled it. Do not dare to take her part in this matter, my child!' The grey eyes, sunk deep now in their sockets, flashed from the thin hawk face.

'I had never dreamed of doing so,' replied Elfleda proudly, stung into anger too, that the Holy Mother could think that she might for a moment condone the queen's behaviour. 'I know that her marriage vows were binding and sacred upon her, and that her vocation could wait. I do not defend her, but only try to explain how this state of affairs came about. Nor do I know how great a part in it Wilfrid played. I was not defending him to you on this score.'

She stopped. She had never meant their conversation to take this turn, and Hilda made no reply. There was a fraught silence, and the daughters of Woden, who dearly loved one another, struggled to subdue the flame of anger that sometimes leapt between them. Hilda leaned back against the wall in weariness, and Elfleda wished that she had not made her angry. She was increasingly concerned about the exhaustion that sometimes overcame her Holy Mother. She upbraided herself bitterly and resolved, not for the first time, that she would not try again to bring Hilda to an understanding of Wilfrid. She had hoped that she might bring them together, and that Wilfrid would defend himself against Hilda's charges with his undoubted eloquence and charm and bring about an understanding at last, and the fruitful exchange of ideas that she knew could spring between them. But it could never be.

Hilda sighed and turned and looked with deep tenderness

131

again at Elfleda and determined to rejoice in the firmness of character that she was beginning to show, and the wisdom that was in her although she was barely twenty. And she had a charm that won all hearts and smoothed the path before her, and above all an openness, a lack of prejudice on every issue, that would be a regenerative force in bringing together the forces that divided the Church. With humility Hilda resolved to renew her own search for such an openness. Only, and the flame of anger flared again, Wilfrid she could never be reconciled with.

Egfrid was a true Anglo-Saxon warrior king of the old tradition, and in the years following his succession he won spectacular victories against the Pictish tribes to the north and the Mercians to the south, extending his kingdom and, as a result, the size of Wilfrid's diocese. His deteriorating relationship with his bishop was not improved by his remarriage, which took place soon after Etheldreda's departure into the monastery at Coldingham. The new queen, Iuminburgh, shared her lord's ambitions and incited him to further jealousy of Wilfrid by describing in detail the bishop's temporal glories: his wealth in both land and possessions, the number of his monasteries, the vastness of their buildings, and his countless followers arrayed and armed as magnificently as the king's own retinue.

Together the king and queen arrived at a means of destroying Wilfrid's power. Messengers were sent to archbishop Theodore in Kent suggesting that the now unwieldy diocese of Northumbria should be split up, making for easier administration and opportunity for the preferment of other ecclesiastics. Theodore visited the north in AD 678, and seeing the logic of the king's suggestion, if not the jealousy that lay behind it, he divided Wilfrid's see into three parts, deposing without consultation the bishop himself who happened to be absent at the time.

Before taking this action Theodore consulted with leaders in the church in Northumbria. Among them was the abbess of Whitby, who gave him her unqualified support. Wilfrid received only his deserts and two of her leading scholars were ordained bishop: Bosa went to the province of Deira with his seat at York, where he supplanted Wilfrid himself, and John to Bernicia, which he shared with Eata who was made Bishop of Lindisfarne, with his seat at Hexham. At the same time Theodore created a new diocese in the conquered Mercian province of Lindsey.

Elfleda was angered and distressed by the injustice done to Wilfrid, and glad when she heard that he had at once set off for Rome, to put his case before the Pope. But she had no heart to raise the matter with Hilda, for all that concerned her by this time was the increasing frailty of her holy Mother. There was no respite from the frequent bouts of fever that she had suffered for some years and these were accompanied now by acute internal pain. Yet for two more years the abbess continued to minister to her flock, and accepted her suffering with a tranquil faith that gave strength and courage to all who were themselves in any distress.

It was AD 680. In the spring-time of the year died Caedmon the herdsman, father of English poetry, and it is not known to this day if the poem that is called 'The Dream of the Rood', that is among the greatest written in the English tongue, whose words are carved in stone upon the cross of Ruthwell, came from his hand.

Enfleda brought the tidings to the dying abbess: told her

how Caedmon had known that his time had come and asked for a bed to be prepared for him in the house set aside for those thought likely to die; how those about him were surprised, for he did not seem sick and conversed with them cheerfully; how soon after midnight he asked for the Eucharist to be placed in his hands, and made his peace with those about him, and waited to hear the brothers chanting the Night office, then made the sign of the cross and laid his head upon the pillow and so died.

'Caedmon,' murmured the abbess, her eyes filling with tears, 'Caedmon. God gave you the time that you needed. You knew when your part in his design was finished.'

For Hilda too the threads were shortening. The sister house at Hackness was established, with Frigyth as prioress. Begu had bowed her head in sad obedience to the Mother's will that she must leave her side, and worked with ceaseless toil so that the weaving workshop should be worthy of the trust placed in her. Hilda knew that her royal successors would continue her work: that the changes that they would initiate would not to any great degree alter her rule and traditions. She did not know that Wilfrid had come back: that the council called in Rome to decide his case had found in his favour and ordered that he must be reinstated, and the bishops who had supplanted him replaced by others. She did not know that the king and his advisors refused to pay any respect to these findings and arrested and imprisoned the bishop on his return.

It was recounted by visiting monks how a violent storm had driven Wilfrid's party to seek refuge on the Frisian coast at the outset of his journey to Rome, and how he had spent the winter months converting the people there and founding a mission in the Netherlands before he resumed his journey. Elfleda shook her head over him in sorrow; a man so gifted, working selflessly and ceaselessly for the Church, always putting the changes of fortune to God's advantage; why did he inspire such enmity, as well as such devotion? She judged it best that the tranquillity of Hilda's last days should not be disturbed by hearing of matters that, Elfleda knew, would disturb and distress her.

Then the threads of the abbess's life ran out. The pattern was complete. In November of that year – AD 680 – her last day came. At about cockcrow she received the Viaticum of the holy communion, and when she had summoned all the servants of Christ in the monastery, she urged them to maintain the Gospel peace among themselves and with others. And while she was still speaking, she joyfully welcomed death, and, in the words of her Lord, passed through it into life.

Then it was granted to Begu that Hilda's death was revealed to her in a vision, so that everyone in the community, even those at a distance in the sister house of Hackness, should know of her death at the same time. As she was resting in the sisters' dormitory, Begu suddenly heard the familiar note of the bell that used to wake and call the nuns to prayer at Whitby when one of their number had died. Opening her eyes, as she thought, she saw the roof open, and a great light pour in from above. While she gazed into this light she saw the soul of God's servant Hilda borne up to heaven in the midst of the light accompanied and guided by angels. Then she awoke, and seeing the other sisters lying around her, realised that what she had seen was either a dream or a vision. Rising at once in alarm, she ran to Frigyth, the prioress, and with many sighs and tears told her that their Mother the abbess Hilda had departed this life, and that she had seen her surrounded by angels in a great light, and ascending to the abode of eternal light to join the company of the saints in heaven. When she had heard the nun's story Frigyth roused all the sisters, and when she had gathered them into the church, she enjoined them to pray and recite the psalter for the soul of their Mother. They did this for the remainder of the night, and at daybreak some brothers arrived from the monastery where she had died with news of her passing. The sisters replied that they already knew, and when they explained how and when they had heard it, it was evident that her death had been revealed to them by means of the vision at the very hour that the brothers said she had died.

It was also said that the same vision came to a sister who served in the house of the novices at Whitby, that was set some distance away from the monastery, a nun who loved the abbess very dearly, so that those in her charge in the same way might know immediately when the Holy Mother died.

The body of the abbess lies upon a bier before the altar in the monastery church of Saint Peter. The monks and nuns of her community file past to make their last farewells. Some have been with her for very many years, and understand the events that have shaped her life.

They recall her proud ancestry, and the dangers of her early years that so quickly formed her courage and independence and led to her swift maturing. They remember the long years of her secular occupation, and her affinity with the Irish traditions of Christian doctrine as the sense of her calling grew within her. They wonder afresh at the exacting task that she at length accomplished in making her monastery a place of learning as well as a haven for the sick and poor.

They know the bitter struggles that she had to undergo: that led to her decision to stay with Edwin's people after his death when she could have escaped to Kent, to the obedient reversal of her long-cherished plan to join her sister in Chelles when Aidan required it of her, and to her acceptance of Oswy's decision, at the synod of Whitby, against the traditions that she loved.

They see that the ravages of those struggles, and of her sickness, have been wiped away. The noble features are as smooth as ivory. The face of the abbess Hilda is the face of a saint.

The gales of autumn lash the fierce waves of the cold North Sea against the granite cliff of Whitby. The earth that will receive the body of the abbess is frozen and still, the life that shall come to birth in the spring sunk deep within it in the sleep of winter. All things are accomplished and the pattern of Hilda's life is woven within the enduring design of the living Church.

EPILOGUE

In the same year that the abbess Hilda died, the year AD 680, the seven-year-old Bede began his education at the monastery of Wearmouth, studying among the books that Benedict Biscop, its founder and abbot, had collected from Gaul and from Rome for his great library. Bede would be the first to translate a part of the scriptures into the Anglo-Saxon tongue, and without his writings nothing would be known about Hilda, and little about the times in which she lived.

In the following year Wilfrid was released from his imprisonment by Egfrid, on condition that he left Northumbria. He found refuge with the Christian king of the South Saxons, Ethelwalh by name, who gave him the estate of Selsey as the seat of a diocese for the kingdom, and during the next five years Wilfrid converted these still pagan people with his characteristic zeal. Then Ethelwalh was murdered by the exiled West Saxon king, Caedwalla, and Caedwalla gave Wilfrid a large part of the Isle of Wight and the task of conversion there. But in the year AD 685 Egfrid, king of Northumbria, was slain in battle against the Picts at Nech-tanesmere, and Wilfrid thought it safe to return and again seek justice, and reinstatement to his bishopric and estates. First he was reconciled with Theodore, the archbishop, who expressed regret at the injustices done to Wilfrid, knowing himself partly to blame. In reparation he wrote on Wilfrid's behalf to Aldfrith, half-brother to Egfrid and his successor, and to the new king's half-sister Elfleda, now abbess of Whitby, and to Ethelred, king of Mercia. Then Wilfrid was permitted to return to his monastery at Ripon as bishop, but without the power throughout Northumbria that he had once enjoyed from his bishopric of York and that for the rest of his life he would struggle to regain.

Until AD 690 he remained peaceably at Ripon, then raised again the question of his bygone power so that Aldfrith and the leaders of the church were roused to anger and once more banished him.

Twice more Wilfrid appealed to Rome for justice, once by proxy, but once again in person enduring the long and arduous journey there from the coast of nothern Gaul, and a near-fatal sickness as he was returning. Each time the force of his arguments won him vindication by the papacy, but each time the councils held to judge his case on his return to Northumbria were torn by bitter controversy between his enemies and those who loved him well and saw no fault in him.

In the year AD 704 King Aldfrith died. And in the same year died Enfleda, joint abbess with her daughter Elfleda of the monastery of Whitby.

Then Wilfrid, an old man now, and no longer in danger from Aldfrith, at last abandoned his dream of restoration to the see of York, and returned to Northumbria and was vindicated and reinstated to his churches of Ripon and Hexham by the judgement of a synod, called by the archbishop who had succeeded Theodore and held beside the river Nidd. The council was swayed in Wilfrid's favour by the eloquence of the abbess Elfleda, who witnessed to Aldfrith's promise on his deathbed that the rulings of the papacy concerning Wilfrid must be obeyed.

After four years of peaceful resignation Wilfrid died in the AD 709, during a visit to the monastery that he had founded at Oundle in the province of the Middle Angles.

In the year AD 686, Egfrid, king of Northumbria, and Theodore, archbishop of Canterbury, had called upon Cuthbert to leave the Inner Farne and again take part in the active life of the Church. So deeply was Cuthbert loved and respected thoughout the kingdom, for his holiness and wisdom, that they wished him to serve as bishop of Hexham while he still had strength to do so. With reluctance he left his solitude, but soon was able to exchange his see with Eata for that of Lindisfarne, so that he might remain close to the retreat that he loved. For two years he carried out the duties of a bishop, preaching and teaching throughout the diocese, with a dignity and ceremony that he thought suitable to his office but with no outward ostentation except for the rare and beautiful pectoral cross that was fashioned for him, and that can be seen to this day. At its heart lay a shell from the Indian ocean, and such was the skill of the setting, from layers of jewelled beading and dog-toothed ornament and stepped cloisonnè work, that it glowed and shimmered with extraordinary light upon his breast and drew all eyes, so that the people knew him as their bishop despite the rough monk's habit that he wore.

Then Cuthbert, knowing that death approached him, sought again his retreat upon the Inner Farne, and there died in AD 687. And it was his greatest wish that there he would be buried, only his monks persuaded him before his death that this could not be. And his body was borne by boat to Lindisfarne and met there by choirs of sweet singers and by a great crowd of the people, and it was buried with ceremony in a stone coffin on the right-hand side of the altar in the monastery church of St Peter. And when in later years the coffin was opened the body of the saint was found in it uncorrupted.

Bishop Edbert succeeded Cuthbert for eleven years, and at his death the priest Edfrith was made bishop; Edfrith who so long ago had looked with love upon the girl Elfleda; Edfrith who at Lindisfarne before he was made bishop had made the Gospels Book that bears its name, for God and for St Cuthbert. And in AD 714 the news was brought to him that the abbess Elfleda had died at Whitby. And by this time the book was finished, and it lay in its glory upon the high altar, within a cover adorned with gold and silver gilt and gems, wrought by an anchorite named Bilfrith. Its text is the Latin of St Jerome's Vulgate, written in the script called insular majuscule, that derived from early Christian Ireland and that Edfrith had brought to perfection.

In its pages the symbols of Christianity weave into the motifs of pagan art; Christian symbols of Mediterranean ancestry that can be traced to Syrian gospel books, to Coptic bindings and Armenian manuscripts, to a Bible decorated a century before in Italy and to the carved ivories of Italian book covers; pagan motifs that reach back through the patterns of Irish metalwork, though the jewellery designs of the Anglo-Saxons and of distant races in the East, to the European roots that the tribes of Britain shared with their invaders. The whorls and coils of pagan art decorate the great initial letters at the beginning of each gospel, and for the carpet pages that precede them Edfrith released a miracle of burgeoning life; beast and bird and plant in spiralling curves; legs and wings, beaks and branches and tails in apparent confusion like the tangle of summer hedgerows, but in a strictly ordered repetition of underlying design that lies against the background of a cross. In the crucible of Edfrith's imagination they were forged into a synthesis, a celebration of God's creation of matter and of every living thing.

And in the Church a synthesis was taking place. The threads of the Roman and Celtic traditions and of their tributary branches were drawing together. The diversity that brought such a flowering of culture to the Northumbrian monasteries had become a unity. Augustine and Columba: Paulinus, Aidan and Hilda: Wilfrid, Elfleda and Cuthbert: in the fast growing church of the emerging English nation they were made one.

141

BIBLIOGRAPHY

The Anglo-Saxon Chronicle translated by G. N. Garmonsway (Dent, 1933).

Sir Frank Stenton, *Anglo-Saxon England* (O.U.P., 1943).

Henry Mayr-Harting, *The Coming of Christianity to Anglo-Saxon England* (Batsford, 1972).

Charles Thomas, *Celtic Britain* (Thames and Hudson, 1986).

Charles Thomas, *Britain and Ireland in Early Christian Times* (Thames and Hudson, 1971).

Nora Chadwick, *The Celts* (Penguin, 1970).

Janet Backhouse, *The Lindisfarne Gospels* (Phaidon, 1981).

D. H. Farmer, *The Oxford Dictionary of Saints* (O.U.P., 1978).

Salway, *Roman Britain* (O.U.P., 1981).

Ian Finlay, *Columba* (Gollancz, 1979).

The Rule of St Benedict translated by David Parry (D.L.T. 1984).

Britain in the Dark Ages (Ordnance Survey, 1966).

The Earliest English Poems translated by Michael Alexander (Penguin, 1966).

Henry Chadwick, *The Early Church* (Penguin, 1967).

R. Bruce-Mitford, *The Sutton Hoo Ship Burial* (British Museum, 1968).

David Wilson, *The Anglo-Saxons* (Penguin, 1971).

H. Ellis Davidson, *Gods and Myths of Northern Europe* (Penguin, 1964).

Dorothy Whitlock, *The Beginnings of English Society* (Penguin, 1952).

The Book of Kells selected by Peter Brown (Thames and Hudson, 1980).

Peter Hunter-Blair, *Northumbria in the Days of Bede* (Gollancz, 1976).

Henry Marsh, *Dark Age Britain* (David and Charles, 1970).

St Wilfrid of Hexham (ed. D. P. Kirby). (Oriel Press, 1974).

Christine Fell, *Women in Anglo-Saxon England* (British Museum publications).

Celt and Saxon, studies in the early British border: ed. N. Chadwick.

Two lives of St. Cuthbert: (ed. Colgrave). (Cambridge).

C. Peers and C. A. Ralegh Radford, *Archeologia, Vol. 89: The Saxon Monastery at Whitby; a report of the 1924 excavation*.

Magnus Backes and Regina Dolling, *Art in the Dark Ages* (Harry Abrams, 1969).

Brian Branston, *The Lost Gods of England* (Thames and Hudson, 1957).

The Earliest life of Gregory the Great translated by B. Colgrave. (C.U.P., 1968).

Lives of the Saints ed. Betty Radice, translated J. F. Webb (Penguin, 1965).

APPENDIX 1

The Romano-British population encountered by the Anglo-Saxon invaders was almost certainly already largely Christian, but these natives did not, perhaps could not, attempt to evangelise the pagan newcomers, whose proud warrior princes laid claim to the ancestry of Woden and the northern gods.

The faith of the British people and of their Irish neighbours, for which the very general term Celtic has come to be used, had grown from many sources. First there was the earliest British church, founded upon the new and growing faith that the Romans brought into the country, along with other cults. Its first martyr was the Roman soldier Alban who died at some time in the third century. By the year AD 314 it was structured enough to send four of its bishops to the Council of Arles, and a century later to be so concerned in theological debate that it sent delegates to Gaul requesting support against the Pelagian heresy, which transgressed the doctrine of original sin and had become rife in Britain. The strong episcopal organisation developed by the British church extended into Wales.

It was not until the early fifth century that monasticism, on any scale, grew out of the anchorite movement whose monks made their way to Ireland and the west from Gaul and the Mediterranean countries, in a search for the ascetic life that had been followed in the Egyptian deserts by Christian fugitives from the persecutions in Rome. These monks set up small, sometimes individual, monastic settlements in the west, organised for their own austere way of life and for the needs of the remote and rugged tribes which they began to serve. The movement was not, however, all in one direction, for they maintained close links with Gaul, and monks from Britain and

144

Ireland made missionary journeys to the continent. Important in this respect was St Columbanus, an Irish monk who, with twelve companions, left Ireland for Gaul in AD 590, attracted a large following there, and founded several monasteries where his monks lived according to Irish traditions. These traditions Columbanus stoutly defended to Pope Gregory, because of the opposition that he met from the Frankish church, as being founded upon more ancient and unsullied sources than those used in some other parts of Christendom. Celtic usages mingled with those of Rome in parts of the continent therefore, and Columbanus established a rather harsh Rule that became widely used, until it was superseded by that of St Benedict. It is possible that Hilda based her Rule upon it at Hartlepool and Whitby, but without its more extreme austerities.

These Celtic monks fully acknowledged the Pope as their head. Their bishops were properly ordained by the laying on of hands through the apostolic succession, and they were orthodox, according to their lights, in matters of ritual and organisation, and in so far as they could be so without easy access to new rulings from Rome. It is significant that Gregory the Great, when instructing Augustine before he left on his mission to the Anglo-Saxons in AD 597, insisted that sympathy and respect must be shown for the forms of Christianity that he would find already existing among the British.

Yet undoubtedly these monks developed different and very individual forms of ecclesiastical organisation and their links with Rome were tenuous and even sometimes questionable, as St Wilfrid, who in the seventh century refused ordination at their hands, clearly thought.

Sometimes Celtic and Roman traditions in Britain met and compromised. In the sixth century mission from Iona to the southern Picts of mainland Britain, Columba's form of monasticism encountered, and became linked with, the diocesan organisation of the British church established by the British bishop Ninian two hundred years earlier. Like that of the Roman church this organisation allowed wide powers of administration to the bishop in his diocese, unlike the Celtic bishop who lived as a monk and was subject to the abbot of his monastery in administrative matters, and whose duties were entirely pastoral and spiritual. In southern Ireland Columban monasticism became merged with the ecclesiastical structure left there by Patrick's mission in the fifth century. Patrick was a Roman Briton, with contacts, after his escape from slavery in Ireland, with the continent and perhaps with Rome itself. He left in the south of Ireland an establishment that was nearer to Roman traditions and that came to accept the Roman dating of Easter, and other controversial matters of doctrine and practice, long before these issues between the Roman and Celtic churches were finally settled at the Synod of Whitby in AD 664.

Customs observed by churches closer to Rome were themselves far from uniform. In Gaul the temporal power and ostentatious wealth of its bishops, who were landowners of noble descent, was an accepted part of ecclesiastical structure there. This considerably influenced Wilfrid, but was not necessarily in accord with practices in Rome where Gregory, for one, advocated an ascetic and simple way of life that had something in common with the monastic rules of the Celtic saints.

The strands of Irish monasticism, and of mainland British and continental customs in the Church, interweave too closely for separation, and the terms Celtic and Roman only loosely define the two sides that faced one another at Whitby when the various issues had polarised. It might not be too much of a generalisation to say that they represented a division that there will always be in the way that people understand their faith, and that is the subject of debate again in our own time, between those who insist on clear doctrinal definition, and those who accept that there are areas of mystery that defy definition in human terms and must always remain ambiguous and open to individual interpretation. It is in some ways part of the age-long tension and debate between the rational and the intuitive.

After Whitby nearly a thousand years would pass before such matters again came to a head, far more drastically and for quite different reasons, at the Reformation.

Appendix 2

The Dream of the Rood
Translated from the Anglo-Saxon by Helen Gardner

Listen! I will tell the most treasured of dreams,
A dream that I dreamt the deep middle of the night,
After the race of men had gone to their rest.
It seemed to me I saw the strangest of Trees,
Lifted aloft in the air, with light all around it,
Of all Beams the brightest. It stood as a beacon,
Drenched in gold; gleaming gems were set
Fair around its foot; five such flamed
High upon its cross-branch. Hosts of angels gazed on it
In world-without-end glory. This was no felon's gallows.
Holy souls in heaven hailed it with wonder
And mortal men on earth and all the Maker wrought.
Strange was that Tree of Triumph – and I a transgressor,
Stained by my sins. I saw the Tree of Glory
Bright with streaming banners, brilliantly shining,
Gilded all with gold. Glittering jewels
Worthily adorned the Tree of the World's Ruler.
Yet beneath the gold I glimpsed the signs
Of some ancient agony when again as of old
Its right side sweated blood. Sorrow seized me;
I was full of fear. I saw the beacon flicker,
Now dazzling, now darkened; at times drenched and dripping
Running red with blood, at times a royal treasure.
Yet even so I lay there for a long while,
Sorrowing at the sight of my Saviour's Tree;
When on a sudden I heard it speak;
The precious wood uttered these words:

'Many years ago – the memory abides –
I was felled to the ground at the forest's edge,
Severed from my roots. Enemies seized me,
Made of me a mark of scorn for criminals to mount on;
Shoulder-high they carried me and set me on a hill.
Many foes made me fast there. Far off then I saw
The King of all mankind coming in great haste,
With courage keen, eager to climb me.
I did not dare, against my Lord's dictate,
To bow down or break, though I beheld tremble
The earth's four corners. I could easily
Have felled his foes; yet fixed and firm I stood.
Then the young Hero – it was God Almighty –
Strong and steadfast, stripped himself for battle;
He climbed up on the high gallows, constant in his purpose,
Mounted it in sight of many, mankind to ransom.
Horror seized me when the Hero clasped me,
But I dared not bow or bend down to earth,
Nor falter, nor fall; firm I needs must stand.
I was raised up a Rood, a royal King I bore,
The High King of Heaven: hold firm I must.
They drove dark nails through me, the dire wounds still show,
Cruel gaping gashes, yet I dared not give as good.
They taunted the two of us; I was wet with teeming blood,
Streaming from the warrior's side when he sent forth his spirit.
High upon that hill helpless I suffered
Long hours of torment; I saw the Lord of Hosts
Outstretched in agony; all embracing darkness
Covered with thick clouds the corpse of the World's Ruler;
The bright day was darkened by a deep shadow,
All its colours clouded; the whole creation wept,
Keened for its King's fall; Christ was on the Rood
Yet warriors from afar eagerly came speeding
To where he hung alone. All this I beheld.
Sore sorrow seized me, yet I stooped to men's hands
Humbly, but with courage keen. They clasped Almighty God,
Raised him from the rack; me they let remain,
Standing soaked in blood, wounded by sharp arrows.
They laid his wearied limbs on earth; the watchers at his head
Looked down on the Lord of Heaven, lying there at rest

Forspent from his great fight. Then they framed for him a tomb
Shaped it of bright stone in the sight of me who slew him.
They laid in it the Lord of Victories, then raised the loud
    lament,
Sang at the sunsetting, then sadly turned away,
Left their glorious Lord. Alone he lay and rested there.
But we three weeping for a long while yet
Stood at our stations as there sank into silence
The cry of the warriors. The corpse grew cold.
The soul's sweet dwelling-place. Us they then struck down,
Felled us all to earth, awful was our fate.
They dug a deep pit, deep down they buried us;
Yet even there the Lord's friends, his faithful thanes found
    me.
With gleaming gold and silver they made me glorious.

The BRITISH ISLES
at the time of ST HILDA

PICTS

SCOTS

Iona

Dumbarton · Inchkeith
Penneltun · Abercorn · Coldingham
BERN · Lindisfarne
Melrose · ICIA · Bamburgh
Yeavering · Alne
BRIT · NORTHUMBRIANS
Hexham · Tyne · Jarrow
Carlisle · Gateshead · Monkwearmouth
Whithorn · ONS · Wear · Hartlepool
Derwentwater · Gilling · Tees · Whitby
Catterick
DEIRA · Lastingham
Ripon · Goodmanham
I. of Man · York · Beverley
Leeds · Humber
Barrow
Hatfield · LINDSEY
Littleboro' · Bardney
Lincoln · Partney

Armagh

Durrow

Anglesey · Chester
Bangor · MERCIANS · Trent
Oswestry · Stamford · GYRWAS · Burgh Castle
Lichfield · Peterborough · EAST
MIDDLE · Oundle · Ely · ANGLES
ANGLES · Dunwich
Bredon · Rendlesham
Caerleon · HWICCAS · EAST
Malmesbury · Thames · Hertford · SAXONS
St Albans · Hatfield · Ythancaestir
WEST · Dorchester · London · Barking · Reculver
SAXONS · Reading · Rochester · Thanet
Chertsey · Canterbury · Richborough
Winchester · SOUTH · KENT
Stoneham · Meon · SAXONS
Redbridge · Bosham · Ambleteus
Selsey · Boulogne
Solent · I. of Wight · Etaples

BRITONS

GAUL

I STEP, I MOUNT: THE VISION OF JOHN HENRY NEWMAN

Edited by Robert Van de Weyer and Pat Saunders

In this selection of extracts, with an extended biographical introduction, we look at the life, ideas and poetry of Cardinal Newman. An Anglican for the first half of his life, Newman became the spiritual leader of the Oxford Movement, seeking sacramental renewal in the Anglican Church. In 1845, he became a Roman Catholic and set out to raise the importance of the laity in the eyes of that church.

THE SPIRITUAL KISS: THE VISION OF SAINT AELRED OF RIEVAULX

Edited by Robert Van de Weyer and Pat Saunders

In this third volume in the Vision of . . . series, the life of Aelred, the official biographer of Edward the Confessor, is considered in the light of his writing. He was a writer in the mystical tradition, severe in his interpretation of the monastic rule but with a genius for friendship. The 'spiritual kiss' to which the title refers is given 'not by the touch of the mouth but by the affection of the heart'.

HIDDEN HEROES OF THE GOSPELS
Feminine Counterparts of Jesus

Joseph A. Grassi

In this fascinating new book, Joseph Grassi studies the Gospels as narrative drama, and discovers that the ideal disciple is often portrayed as a woman. Pursuing a detailed analysis of the literary structure of each of the four Gospels, Grassi shows how the text works to point out the model forms of discipleship, and how women fit this model. Among the women portrayed are the poor widow in the Temple, the daughter of Jairus, the Syro-Phoenician woman, and Mary Magdalene. £4.99

A NON-VIOLENT LIFESTYLE
Conversations with Jean and Hildegard Goss-Mayr

Gérard Houver

Jean and Hildegard Goss-Mayr have spent their lives spreading abroad their message of non-violence. Nominated for the Nobel Peace Prize, they have given seminars throughout the world. £4.99

DRAW NEAR TO GOD
Daily Meditations with Pope John Paul II

In daily meditations throughout the church year, the Pope reflects on the place of marriage, family and work in the Christian's life. He challenges all Christians to respect life, to evangelise and to bring the peace of Christ to a weary world. £4.99

THE WARSAW GHETTO
A Christian's Testimony

Wladyslaw Bartoszewski

Wladyslaw Bartoszewski, a Roman Catholic, offers here a rare testimony to the shared fate of Warsaw's inhabitants during the Holocaust of World War II. His unique and moving book tells the story of the Warsaw ghetto from the unusual perspective of one of the few ethnic Poles to have come to the aid of the Jews during the war. At great peril to his own life, he worked to save some of the Jews and to publicise the events taking place in Poland to an unbelieving world.